# Southwest Slow Cooking

## by Tammy Biber and Theresa Howell

Photography by Christopher Marchetti

Northland Publishing

www.northlandbooks.com

Composed in the United States of America
Printed in China

Edited by Kathleen Bryant
Designed by Katie Jennings
Production supervised by Donna Boyd
Index compiled by Jan Williams, Indexing Services

We would like to offer a special thank you to Mary Gales for letting us photograph her beautiful kitchen accessories,
to Aunt Maude of Aunt Maude's Antique Mall for letting us photograph her unique antiques,
to George Averbeck of Fire on the Mountain Gallery for letting us photograph his handblown glass chiles,
and to Lisa Aguiñaga-Mansfield of De Colores del Barrio for letting us photograph her authentic Mexican wares.

FIRST IMPRESSION 2004
ISBN 0-87358-856-8

05  06  07  08  09        6  5  4  3  2

Library of Congress Cataloging-in-Publication Data

Biber, Tammy, 1971-
Southwest Slow Cooking / by Tammy Biber and Theresa Howell ; photography by Christopher Marchetti.
p. cm.
1. Cookery, American—Southwestern style. 2. Electric cookery, Slow. I. Howell, Theresa, 1974- II. Title.

TX715.2.S68B53 2004
641.5'884—dc22         2004049596

To my loving husband, Dave,
who has turned every challenging experience this year
into an exciting adventure.
—TAB

To my wonderful husband, Brian,
my number-one taste tester.
You are my inspiration and my very best friend.
—TAH

Carne 73

Vegetariano 87

Pan y Postres 105

Antojitos 7

# Contents

# Introduction

The slow cooker is back and, in all its glory, is more popular than ever. Are you surprised? It only makes sense. There has never been a more accommodating, easy-to-use kitchen appliance that has the ability to make your life easier, while providing the means to cook up an amazing meal. In a world where we are constantly on the go and mealtime can so easily get pushed aside or popped in the microwave, the slow cooker brings us back to home cooking.

While working on this cookbook, we found that there are countless people whose thoughts linger on the ol' pot roast and potatoes that repeatedly appeared out of their mother's tangerine-colored "crock." Well, we have never been your typical meat-and-potatoes type of women. Our palates are accustomed to the wonderfully diverse flavors of the Southwest. One of our goals in writing this cookbook is to dispel those age-old myths surrounding the all-mighty slow cooker. We're here to bring new life to this amazing appliance and show everyone that the slow cooker can be exciting, adventurous, and creative, especially when used to prepare southwestern fare!

The truth is, we have unabashedly fallen in love with the energy, tradition, and spice of the flavors of the Southwest. Give us a tortilla over a slice of bread any day! Our kitchens are stocked with red chile sauces, roasted green chiles, fresh Mexican cheeses, salsa, pintos, poblanos, and cilantro. These flavors are not new, but they are exciting—they sing and dance with zest and tang, the true essence of the Southwest. Southwestern cuisine encompasses influences from Mexican, Native American, and even cowboy-style cooking. It is a full-flavored blend of cultures, but what southwestern cooking so often means is spending hours in the kitchen. It exemplifies the original definition of *sloooow* cooking.

Not only do we love the flavors of the Southwest, we love the landscape from which they were born—the deserts, mountains, and forests. We're active, working women who get outdoors and explore this amazing region of the country every chance we get. So we had to do something creative to be able to enjoy the authentic, slow-cooked flavors of the Southwest that we love so dearly without turning down opportunities to put in that extra mile at work, hike in the gorgeous outdoors, cross-country ski, or just relax in the southwestern sun. Hmmm… hike or spend the weekend in the kitchen? Something had to be done. You've guessed it— the slow cooker has come to our rescue.

What you'll find in this cookbook are 101 Southwest recipes exploding with flavor that come straight from everyone's favorite kitchen appliance—the slow cooker. This means that from now on, you can take off for that day hike on the mountain but still come home to a house that smells of warmth and goodness. So, while you're out doing a million things in one day, whether it's working or playing, your slow cooker is doing the supremely important job of cooking a hearty meal that is ready when you are. You've got to love that! Dinner is served.

# The Southwest Kitchen

We are lucky to live in the Southwest! The three-hundred-plus days of sunshine, easy access to endless wilderness for recreation, and almost year-round fresh ingredients make this, in our opinion, one of the best places to live in the country. And, when all of these qualities are combined in a culinary manner, the results are unique, flavorful dishes inspired by the ancient cultures that inhabit our region.

In order to successfully recreate the variety of southwestern-style dishes included in this book, your kitchen will require a staple of ingredients. In some cases, you might find that it is easier to substitute some of the following ingredients for more familiar ones, but be assured that using these authentic southwestern flavors will improve the taste and atmosphere of your meal.

## Chiles

The first and foremost ingredient in any southwestern dish is the chile. Most people are familiar with typical chile varieties such as jalapeños and green chiles, but there are so many delicious kinds now available in most supermarkets that it is a shame to be relegated to only two. So, to help widen your chile horizon, we've included a variety of different chiles in our recipes for you to sample.

There are a couple of facts to be aware of when including chiles in your cooking. First, chiles come in two main forms: fresh and dried. In each form, they typically have a different name. For example, jalapeños become chipotles and poblanos become anchos, and depending on what part of the country you are in, there may be some discrepancy in these names. Also, you will find that even these two forms are offered in different ways. For example, you will see roasted chiles in many of our recipes. You can buy chiles in cans that have been roasted, you can roast your own chiles under a hot broiler or over an open flame until the skin turns black, or, if you are lucky enough to live in the Southwest, you can buy fresh chiles and have them roasted by the bagload right in front of your eyes. The aroma is simply delicious!

Another example, the chipotle, as previously mentioned, is a smoked and dried jalapeño, but it is most often found canned in adobo sauce in the Mexican food section of your local grocery store. And since multiple chipotles come in one can with adobo sauce,

make sure you pay attention to how many chiles are called for in each recipe. Don't make the mistake of throwing in the whole can. You'll find out soon enough if you used too many chiles!

Second, when you add fresh chiles to the slow cooker, the heat will mellow out into a nice, smooth flavor. However, when you add dried chiles to the slow cooker, the heat has a tendency to intensify. Make sure you have experimented with the chiles you are using before deciding to toss in a few more.

Finally, as most people now know, the seeds and membranes found inside a chile are what contain the heat. By removing most or all of the seeds and membranes, you can reduce the heat level. This rule holds true for both the fresh and dried varieties, so decide what is appropriate for your own heat tolerance and adjust accordingly as you cook.

## Cheese

Cheese is another important ingredient in Southwest cooking. Throughout this book, you will find a variety of cheeses. In most cases, you can substitute your favorite cheese for the Mexican variety listed. However, if the Mexican cheese is available, we highly recommend giving it a try. The varieties we like—cotija, quesadilla, ranchero, and panela—to name a few, add a smooth, rich flavor that can't be compared to our American cheeses. If you love cheese, you shouldn't miss these wonderful new flavors.

## Salsa

Since salsa replaced ketchup as the number-one condiment in America a few years ago, we don't need to say much about it. Just remember that salsas don't need to contain dozens of ingredients to be good. Look at the labels on each jar and pick a salsa with as few ingredients as possible. That way, each flavor can present itself without being overpowered by too many other ingredients.

Another option is to make your own salsa. If you have time, salsa is so easy to make. Pick what kind of base you want to use—tomatoes, tomatillos, green chiles—and then add a few of your other favorite ingredients like garlic, onion, and cilantro. Mix your salsa well and let it sit in the refrigerator for at least one hour so that the flavors can blend. Making your own salsa will be a rewarding way to top off your meal.

## Herbs

You will find that quite a number of our recipes call for fresh cilantro as a garnish. Cilantro has a very specific flavor that perfectly complements southwestern food, and it is readily available across the country. If you don't like cilantro, there are a few other ways to top off a good meal without losing its authenticity.

epazote

cilantro

Epazote, an herb found throughout Mexico, is a wonderful ingredient found in many authentic meals. While in cooking school in central Mexico, we used epazote in quite a few dishes. It has a very unique taste that adds depth to Mexican cuisine. However, we were concerned about the availability of this tasty herb at home. If you can't find epazote, Doña Estela, owner of Mexican Home Cooking School in Tlaxcala, suggests throwing a little dill into your dish. You can either add it to the recipe, or use it as a garnish on top. Your guests will be blown away by your creativity, while you will be privy to this authentic Mexican secret.

## Beans

Beans are a staple in many cultures, but they are a must in southwestern cooking. In our recipes, you will see both dried and canned beans, and you may substitute one for the other depending on your preference. What we have found in working with both kinds of beans is that the canned beans are by far the easiest form to use, but they lose a little of their consistency after being cooked all day. The dried beans do take more work, but they will remain nice and tender without giving up their consistency. No matter which form of beans you use, they will add a heartiness and depth to your soups, stews, and chilis.

## Tortillas

There is nothing better than a fresh, hot tortilla served alongside your Southwest meal; however, fresh tortillas can be very difficult to find. We are lucky to have a place in town that delivers homemade tortillas to the local grocery stores…and they go quickly! Look in your local phone book and find out if there is a place in your area that makes homemade tortillas. If there isn't, you can create the effect by microwaving three or four tortillas at a time in an unsealed plastic bag for thirty seconds. Place the heated tortillas in a tortilla warmer or in a folded dishtowel and serve with your meal. You'll be amazed at the difference hot tortillas can make as an accompaniment.

## Beer

All beers are not created equal. When you drink a good Mexican beer, you can just taste the sun, the ocean, and the relaxed pace of life. We use beer in a number of our recipes, and it always tastes best when you use a Mexican variety like Corona, Dos Equis, Negra Modelo, or Tecate. When you are ready to serve your meal, offer your guests the same beer used in the recipe with a little lime, and the cold, crisp beer will enhance the warm, smooth taste in the recipe.

If you take the time to add these basic staples to your pantry, you will find that Southwest cooking will be not only enjoyable, but also flavorful and easy. And this pantry list is just the beginning. As you delve deeper into Southwest cuisine and really explore all the new flavors and tempting tastes it has to offer, the more you'll learn to appreciate it and embrace it as a part of your lifestyle. So, why not start immediately and create a taste of the Southwest in your kitchen—tonight!

# Slow Cooking Tips

The slow cooker is not a complicated appliance. In fact, it's just the opposite. There are, however, a few tips and things to take into consideration that will help you appreciate the benefits of your slow cooker. With a basic understanding of how the slow cooker works and what it can accomplish, you'll understand exactly why they are so popular and practical today.

## Healthy Cooking

The slow cooker naturally lends itself to cooking healthy meals. It is a versatile appliance. It beautifully cooks up vegetables and meat dishes—usually all in the same meal. This makes it easy for you to prepare balanced meals for your family in one easy step. It is also wonderful for preparing balanced vegetarian meals, something that is not usually associated with the slow cooker. One of the most important health benefits of using the slow cooker to prepare meals is that it is not necessary to add additional fats. The slow-cooking method allows the flavors within the ceramic pot to blend and complement each other over the course of many hours without having to add excess oil or butter. Plus, if you are counting carbohydrates, the slow cooker is ideal for preparing high protein, low carb meals that are hearty enough to fill you up without a side of rice or potatoes.

## Economical

Because the slow cooker works all day at tenderizing meats, it is possible to purchase cheaper, tougher cuts of meat. They certainly are not tough after slowly stewing in savory juices for eight hours. Additionally, a little meat goes a long way. In many of the soups and stews, for instance, using two chicken breasts is just enough for four hearty and satisfying servings. Especially in the case of soups, stews, and chilis, you might find that you have enough left over for another lunch or two. On top of it all, the slow cooker is the ultimate energy-saving appliance. If you use your slow cooker enough, you just might notice a dent in your monthly electricity bill.

## Timing

It seems almost counterintuitive that something that takes so long to cook food is so convenient and conducive to our busy lifestyles. What the slow cooker offers us is the opportunity to put together a healthy meal and then walk away. As we like to say, the meal is ready when we are. What we often do is prepare the ingredients the night before, put them in the crockery, cover it with plastic wrap, and then place it in the fridge. That way, before we walk out the door to work in the morning all we have to do put the crockery in the slow cooker and turn it on. Here are a few hints if this is the schedule you choose to follow. First, never mix the meats and the vegetables the night before. You can chop the vegetables and trim the fat off the meat in the evening, but keep them separate until just before you turn on the slow cooker. We also add the liquids as a last step. And second, if you do prepare the ingredients the night before and place your slow cooker in the fridge, cover it with plastic wrap instead of using the glass cover. This will help contain all of the flavors and aromas in the slow cooker, not in the refrigerator. Discard the plastic wrap in the morning and use the glass cover when cooking.

One of our favorite benefits of the slow cooker is that the cooking times indicated are more like guidelines rather than strict rules. If you have to stay late at work, for instance, and the slow cooker is cooking away at home, an extra hour here or there does not hurt at all. It is nearly impossible to burn food in your slow cooker. This gives you more flexibility and allows you to serve dinner when you are ready.

## Two-step recipes

In this book, you will find a handful of recipes that require cooking the meal in the slow cooker all day, then involve another step right before serving such as rolling a burrito, baking a pan of enchiladas, or stuffing a taco. These recipes do take more time than many of our other slow cooker recipes, but when these authentic recipes are prepared the traditional way without the slow cooker, they will still take four to five hours in the oven. Many authentic Southwest meals take time in preparing the main ingredients, so by using the slow cooker instead of the oven, you are saving yourself the time of standing in the kitchen watching the oven slowly cook your meat. Just make sure you figure in some extra time at the end for the last essential steps.

## High vs. Low

These days, many slow cookers have more than the two traditional settings: high and low. However, since we acquired our first slow cookers from our parents—you know, the old brown and olive-green ones with only two settings—we learned to cook using those two standard settings. So even though we gave up those antiques years ago, you will still see those two basic settings used in our recipes.

In most situations, the low setting will be appropriate. However, if you forgot to turn on the delicious meal you had sitting in the refrigerator just waiting to be slow cooked all day, you can kick on the high heat and cook your meal in half the time. A general rule of thumb is that using the high setting cuts the cooking time in half. Typically, the meats will not be as tender as they would be if cooked all day on low. Another scenario for using high heat is if you have reached the end of the meal, and there is just too much liquid in the slow cooker. You can remove the cover, turn up the heat, and let the meal cook this way until most of the excess liquid has evaporated. Some of our egg-based recipes also call for high heat. This allows the meal to brown on the outsides and form a nice thick crust. Both settings have their place, so determine how much time you have and what results you want and choose your heat setting accordingly.

## No Peeking

The slow cooker does not need supervision. That's why it's so perfect. You can just turn it on and do whatever it is you need to do. It's wonderful! However, we do understand the human temptation to peek and meddle with things that should be left alone. Try to resist. Every time you lift the lid, valuable heat escapes, significantly slowing down the cooking process. Except when you're cooking beans, it is usually not necessary to stir. The slow cooker uses indirect heat and therefore cooks whatever is inside evenly. We do recommend, however, putting the vegetables on the bottom of your slow cooker and placing the meat on top. This allows the vegetables to remain submerged in the liquids and cook evenly.

## Dairy

So many slow cooker cookbooks firmly state, "Never use dairy products in the slow cooker." Through our schooling in Mexico and our experiences in the Southwest, we quickly learned that this rule is not exactly true. It *is* a bad idea to put dairy products in the slow cooker with your pot roast that takes seven to eight hours to cook. However, we found that if you add cheese, milk, or sour cream to your meals that only require four to five hours, or if you add the dairy in the last hour of cooking, it can add both flavor and consistency. Cheese will top off your chicken, milk will smooth out your sauces, and sour cream will tone down the spicy bite of chipotle. So while we don't recommend adding dairy for an entire day of cooking, we highly favor adding it at the appropriate time. You will find that many of our recipes call for dairy products, so don't worry about that age-old "no dairy in the slow cooker" rule from your mother's cookbook. You'll be missing out on an amazing variety of creamy textures and rich tastes.

Slow cookers are traditionally known for creating warm, delicious dinners; however, they are also perfect for making an array of appealing appetizers. This chapter contains a variety of recipes, including dips, sauces, and munchies. So the next time you are hosting a party for family or friends, these recipes offer solutions for all your entertaining needs.

 Starters

## Antojitos

Most people are familiar with cold artichoke dip, but this hot version is sure to spice up your party! Serve this dip with a variety of decorative crackers, chips, or fresh bread.

# Hot Artichoke Dip

2 (14-ounce) cans quartered artichoke hearts
1 cup chopped baby spinach
1 tablespoon dried oregano
1 (12-ounce) container whipped cream cheese
1 teaspoon cayenne
1/2 teaspoon garlic powder
3 green chiles, roasted, peeled, and chopped

Mix all ingredients in the slow cooker. Cover and cook on high for 1 hour. Stir, cover, and cook on low for 1 hour more, or until the dip is warmed through. • Makes Approximately 4 Cups

Bring your slow cooker filled with this popular and pleasing dip along to your next party. It'll be gone before you know it.

# Bean & Salsa Dip

Brown the beef in a medium-sized skillet. Drain off the grease, and add the salt, chili powder, cayenne, and garlic. Cook for 2 more minutes. In your slow cooker, combine the beef mixture with the salsa, refried beans, sour cream, and 2 cups of the Cheddar cheese. Cover and cook on low for 2 to 3 hours. Fifteen minutes before serving, sprinkle the remaining cheese on top. Keep the cover off and continue cooking on low to keep the bean dip warm. Serve with tortilla chips. • Makes Approximately 8 Cups

1 pound lean ground beef
1/2 teaspoon salt
1 tablespoon chili powder
1/8 teaspoon cayenne
5 cloves garlic, crushed
2 (16-ounce) jars salsa
1 (15-ounce) can refried beans
1 1/2 cups low-fat sour cream
2 cups plus 1/2 cup shredded
   Cheddar cheese

Sometimes on the weekend, my husband and I will feast on a pot full of this dip in place of lunch.

# Hot Black Bean Dip

Combine all ingredients except the cheese in your slow cooker. Cover and cook on high for 1 hour. Gently smash the beans along the side of the crockery. Sprinkle with the cheese, cover, and cook for 30 minutes more. Serve warm with tortilla chips. • Makes Approximately 4 Cups

2 (15-ounce) cans black beans, drained
1 (10-ounce) can diced tomatoes
   in sauce
3 chipotle chiles in adobo sauce,
   finely chopped
1 tablespoon adobo sauce
3 tablespoons finely chopped onion
1/2 teaspoon dried oregano
2 tablespoons chopped fresh cilantro
1 clove garlic, crushed
Juice of one lime
1/2 cup crumbled feta cheese

Serve this elegant dip with tortilla chips or fresh vegetables.

# Roasted Red Pepper Dip

1 (12-ounce) jar roasted red peppers, drained and chopped
8 ounces Monterey jack cheese, shredded
8 ounces cream cheese, softened
2 tablespoons minced onion
1 clove garlic, crushed
1/2 teaspoon ground cumin
1 cup sour cream

Combine the red peppers, Monterey jack cheese, cream cheese, onion, garlic, and cumin in the slow cooker. Cover and cook on low for 45 minutes. Stir in the sour cream. Cover and continue cooking on low for 15 minutes more. Serve with tortilla chips and fresh vegetables. • Makes Approximately 4 Cups

Note: To keep the dip warm while serving, remove the lid and keep on low. Stir occasionally to prevent the dip from sticking to the sides.

The slow cooker is the perfect way to make and serve fondue. This traditional white cheese recipe was given to me by my aunt, Diane Cavis, and is now a family favorite.

# White Cheese Fondue

1 clove garlic
1/2 pound Gruyère cheese, shredded
1/2 pound Swiss cheese, shredded
1/4 cup all-purpose flour
1/4 teaspoon black pepper
1/4 teaspoon cayenne
1 can chopped green chiles
1 cup dry white wine

Preheat the slow cooker to high. Slightly crush the garlic, and rub it on the inside of the slow cooker. Discard the garlic. In a separate bowl, mix together the cheeses, flour, pepper, cayenne, and chiles. Set aside.

Heat the wine on the stove top until tiny bubbles form. Do not boil. Turn the slow cooker to low, and pour in the heated wine. Immediately add the cheese mixture and stir until melted, about 3 minutes. Keep the fondue warm in the slow cooker until ready to serve, stirring frequently. • Makes Approximately 8 Cups

This colorful and delectable dip is sinfully delicious. It is a good idea to use a fork when scooping the dip onto your chips, and make sure you have plenty of napkins nearby.

# Red, Yellow, & Green Rajas con Queso

Coat the bottom of your slow cooker with 1 tablespoon of the olive oil. Lay the bell pepper strips and garlic slices evenly along the bottom and sides. Drizzle the remaining 1 tablespoon of olive oil over the peppers. Cover and cook on low for 4 hours.

When the peppers strips are soft, drain off some of the extra oil while keeping the peppers and garlic in the slow cooker. Season the peppers with salt and black pepper to taste, and sprinkle with red pepper flakes. Evenly spread the sour cream over the peppers and cover with the cheese. Continue cooking on low with the cover off until the cheese is completely melted, about 5 to 10 minutes. Serve the rajas with cocktail forks and tortilla chips.

• Makes Approximately 1 1/2 Cups

2 tablespoons olive oil
1 red bell pepper, cut into 1/2-inch strips
1 yellow bell pepper, cut into 1/2-inch strips
1 green bell pepper, cut into 1/2-inch strips
2 cloves garlic, thinly sliced
Salt and black pepper
1 teaspoon red pepper flakes
1/2 cup low-fat sour cream
1 cup shredded Cheddar cheese

This chutney is a delicious combination of hot and sweet. It's best when made with freshly roasted green chiles. I love to serve this as an appetizer over cream cheese with crackers, but it can also be used in combination with chicken or pork.

# Green Chile Chutney

2 cups roasted green chiles, seeded and chopped
1 cup sugar
1/2 cup cider vinegar
1 teaspoon ground cumin
1/2 cup finely chopped onion
1 (8-ounce) block cream cheese

Combine all of the ingredients except for the cream cheese in the slow cooker. Cover and cook on low for 4 to 5 hours. Place the cream cheese block on a decorative platter and pour the chutney over the cheese. Serve with crackers on the side.

• Makes Approximately 3 Cups

Dates are plentiful in the Southwest region, but most people aren't quite sure what to do with them. This recipe is simple and yields a delicious spread that will last for two weeks in your refrigerator. Spread it generously on bread, bagels, or muffins.

# Lemon Date Butter

2 cups unsugared dates, seeded and chopped
1 cup raw sugar
1 3/4 cups water
2 tablespoons lemon zest
1/4 cup lemon juice

Combine all of the ingredients in the slow cooker. Cover and cook on low for 6 hours. Remove approximately three-quarters of the heated mixture and transfer it to the blender. Blend for 2 minutes. Return the mixture to the slow cooker and stir until smooth and creamy.

Let the butter cool in the refrigerator for at least 12 hours. Store in an airtight container. • Makes Approximately 4 Cups

I grew up with this tasty little appetizer, as my mom always fixed it for guests at our parties. It wasn't until I got older and started hosting my own parties that I understood just how easy these delicious meatballs are to make. I add a little extra kick to my meatballs, which allows them to live up to their Spanish name—*albóndigas.*

# Albóndigas

Preheat oven to 350° F. Soak the slice of bread in water and squeeze out the liquid. In a medium bowl, mix the bread with the ground beef, egg, salt, black pepper, chipotle powder, and garlic. Using your hands, mix the ingredients until they stick together. Form the meat mixture into tiny meatballs, about 1 inch in diameter. Place the meatballs on a cookie sheet, and bake for approximately 8 to 10 minutes until lightly brown. Remove from the oven and immediately place in the slow cooker. Add the entire bottle of barbecue sauce, cover, and bake for 5 to 6 hours on low.

Approximately 1 hour before you plan to serve the meatballs, mix the cornstarch, sugar, and water in a small bowl. Add to the meatball mixture to thicken the sauce. This will also help the sauce stick to the meatballs. Cover and let warm for 15 minutes more. Remove the meatballs from the slow cooker, place them on a decorative serving platter, drizzle some of the barbecue sauce over the top, and serve individually with toothpicks.

• Makes Approximately 24 Meatballs

1 slice white bread
1 pound lean ground beef
1 egg, slightly beaten
1/4 teaspoon salt
1/4 teaspoon black pepper
1/2 teaspoon chipotle powder
1 clove garlic, crushed
1 (20-ounce) bottle prepared barbecue sauce
2 tablespoons cornstarch
1 tablespoon sugar
1/4 cup water

Since Buffalo wings are named after the city of Buffalo, we thought we'd name these delicious wings after our hometown, the place where this smoky, spicy recipe was created—Flagstaff.

# Flagstaff Wings

1/4 cup margarine, melted
1/2 cup Tabasco® Brand Chipotle Pepper Sauce
1 tablespoon honey
1 tablespoon cider vinegar
1 teaspoon garlic powder
Nonstick cooking spray
1 1/2 pounds chicken wing drummettes

Combine all ingredients except for the chicken wings in a medium-sized bowl. Mix well and set aside.

Brown the wing drummettes in a skillet with nonstick cooking spray, flipping periodically, about 5 minutes. When the drummettes are slightly browned, transfer them to the bowl with the sauce. Gently stir, making sure all chicken wings are evenly covered with the sauce. Transfer the wings and sauce to the slow cooker. Cover and cook on low for 5 to 6 hours, opening at least once during cooking to stir.

When cooked through, remove the wings from the slow cooker and place them on a decorative platter. Drizzle with the sauce, and serve with blue cheese dressing, carrot sticks, and celery sticks. • Makes Approximately 14 Wings

No one will suspect that a slow cooker is behind this fancy appetizer.

# Roasted Red Pepper & Garlic Tostinis

Coat the bottom of the slow cooker with 1 tablespoon of the oil. Cut the top off the head of garlic and place the entire head, minus the top, in the center of the slow cooker. Stack the bell peppers on the bottom of the slow cooker along the edges. Drizzle the remaining 1 tablespoon of oil over the top of the garlic and peppers. Cover and cook on low for 5 hours.

Preheat the oven to 350° F. Place the slices of bread on an ungreased cookie sheet. Squeeze one clove of garlic on each slice of bread, and spread it across the surface. Slice the red peppers and equally distribute them over the tops of each slice of bread. Season each piece with salt and pepper to taste and top with feta cheese. Bake in the oven for 10 minutes, or until the cheese has started to melt. Serve immediately. ● Makes Approximately 16 Tostinis

1 tablespoon plus 1 tablespoon olive oil
1 head garlic
2 red bell peppers, seeded and quartered
1 French baguette, cut into $1/4$-inch slices
Salt and black pepper
$1/2$ cup crumbled feta cheese

A very good friend first walked this dish into my house five years ago. Since then, I've been requesting it every time we have a potluck. You'll need some toothpicks to dig right in. Thanks for your contribution, Gina!

# Western Citrus Sausage

1 onion, chopped
4 large links smoked sausage
1 (12-ounce) can beer
1 (20-ounce) bottle prepared barbecue sauce
1/2 cup ketchup
1/2 cup lightly packed brown sugar
1 tablespoon Worcestershire sauce
1 tablespoon prepared spicy brown mustard
1 orange, sliced
1 lemon, sliced

In a medium-sized pan, cook the onions and sausage in the beer, about 10 minutes. Drain well. Add the remaining ingredients and bring to a boil, stirring constantly. Transfer to the slow cooker, cover, and cook on low for 3 hours. When cooked through, remove the sausage from the slow cooker and slice each link into 4 or 5 pieces. Place the sausage and the sauce from the slow cooker in a decorative bowl and serve. This appetizer is especially good when served with freshly baked bread.
• Makes Approximately 16 Sausage Slices

The slow cooker is best known for its hearty soups, stews, and chilis. Imagine coming home from a long day at work to the aromas of roasted garlic, sweet onions, and warm chiles, all inviting you to sit down and enjoy dinner.

# Soups, Stews, & Chilis

## Sopas

Tortilla Soup
Sopa de Lima
Red Pepper Soup
Chipotle & Garbanzo Bean Soup
Chipotle Lentil Soup
Drowned Egg Soup
Black Bean Soup
Red Posole
Posole Blanco
Sopa de Albóndigas
Crema de Chile Poblano
Sweet Potato & Chipotle Soup
Piñon Soup
Spicy Sausage Soup
Southwest Onion Soup
Green Chile & Garbanzo Bean Stew
Chile Verde
Potato Chile Stew
Red Chile Beef Stew
Chicken Chili
Mexican Flag Chili
Three Bean Vegetarian Chili

This is my favorite recipe; it tastes fresh and new every time. The recipe calls for red chile sauce, which can be found in the Mexican section of most grocery stores. If you cannot find it, a good quality red enchilada sauce will do in a pinch.

# Tortilla Soup

1 onion, finely chopped
1 tablespoon olive oil
3 cloves garlic, crushed
1 jalapeño, seeded and chopped
1 (16-ounce) can diced tomatoes, undrained
2 tablespoons tomato paste
2 green chiles, roasted and chopped
2 teaspoons ground cumin
1/4 teaspoon cayenne
1 tablespoon cornmeal
2 1/2 cups chicken stock
2 cups red chile sauce
2 boneless chicken breasts
1 avocado, pitted, peeled, and diced
2 limes
Cilantro
Monterey jack cheese, shredded
Tortilla chips

Sauté the onions in a skillet with the olive oil. In the slow cooker, combine the sautéed onions, garlic, jalapeño, diced tomatoes, tomato paste, chiles, cumin, cayenne, cornmeal, chicken stock, red chile sauce, and chicken breasts. Cover and cook on low for 5 to 6 hours. Remove chicken, shred with a fork, and return to the slow cooker. Add avocado, cover, and cook on low until soup is thoroughly heated. Spoon soup into individual serving bowls and garnish with lime juice, cilantro, cheese, and tortillas.
• Makes 4-6 Servings

There are so many delicious ingredients in this soup, but the limes get top billing. Adding the juice of a whole lime to each bowl of soup right before serving pulls everything together.

# Sopa de Lima

4 cups chicken stock
2 boneless chicken breasts
3 cloves garlic, crushed
1/2 teaspoon salt
1/2 teaspoon ground cumin
1/4 teaspoon ground cinnamon
1/8 teaspoon ground cloves
1 teaspoon dried oregano
1/4 teaspoon cayenne
1 red onion, chopped
1 green pepper, finely chopped
3 Roma tomatoes, chopped
1 green chile, chopped
2 tablespoons vegetable oil
6 (6-inch) corn tortillas, cut into
1/4-inch strips
1 avocado, pitted, peeled, and chopped
Cilantro
4-6 limes

Place all ingredients except for the avocado, vegetable oil, tortillas, and limes in slow cooker. Cover and cook on low for 6 to 8 hours.

Remove chicken, shred with a fork, and return to the slow cooker. Continue cooking on low until ready to serve.

In the meantime, heat oil in a medium-size skillet. Sauté the tortilla strips until crisp. Spoon soup into individual serving bowls and garnish each with the juice of a whole lime, avocado, cilantro, and tortilla strips. • Makes 4-6 Servings

The roasted red peppers give this soup a tangy, smoky flavor. After blending, you'll have a lovely red soup that goes well with tortillas or bread.

# Red Pepper Soup

1 onion, chopped
3 cloves garlic, chopped
1 1/2 tablespoons olive oil
2 (15-ounce) jars roasted red peppers, drained and chopped
1 (8-ounce) can tomato paste
1/2 cup white wine
1 cup chicken stock
1/2 teaspoon salt
1/2 teaspoon dried oregano
1 tablespoon balsamic vinegar
3 sprigs fresh thyme
1 tablespoon honey
1 cup sour cream
3 tablespoons chopped cilantro

Sauté the onions and garlic in the oil. In the slow cooker, combine all ingredients except for the sour cream and cilantro. Cover and cook on low for 7 to 8 hours.

Transfer soup to a blender, and blend until mostly smooth. Return the blended soup to the slow cooker, and add the sour cream and cilantro. Cover and cook on high for 30 minutes, or until soup is heated through. • Makes 2-4 Servings

This is a good summertime soup. It is light and smoky, and goes well with cold Mexican beer.

# Chipotle & Garbanzo Bean Soup

Combine all ingredients except green onions, cheese, limes, and cilantro in slow cooker. Cover and cook on low for 5 to 7 hours.

Thirty minutes before serving, remove the chicken from the soup, shred, and return to the slow cooker. Add the green onions. Cook on low until ready to serve. Divide the cubed cheese equally into soup bowls. Ladle the soup into bowls over the cheese, add juice from half a lime into each bowl, and garnish with cilantro.

• Makes 4-6 Servings

2 boneless chicken breasts
4 cups chicken stock
2 (15-ounce) cans garbanzo beans, drained and rinsed
2 chipotles in adobo sauce, seeded
2 tablespoons adobo sauce
6 green chiles, chopped
1 teaspoon dried oregano
1 teaspoon garlic powder
3/4 cup chopped green onions
1 cup cubed Monterey jack cheese or queso quesadilla
2 limes
Cilantro

This is a delicious soup that will warm your house on a cold winter day. The lentils make it easy since they don't need to be soaked overnight. If you want a thicker, heartier stew, add an extra cup of lentils.

# Chipotle Lentil Soup

1 cup lentils, picked clean and rinsed
1 cup chopped celery
1 cup chopped carrots
1 yellow onion, chopped
6 cloves garlic, chopped
2-3 chipotles in adobo sauce, seeded and chopped
1 (16-ounce) can corn, drained
3-4 boneless chicken breasts
1 teaspoon dried basil
1 teaspoon dried oregano
1/2 teaspoon dried rosemary
1 teaspoon black pepper
2 bay leaves
4 cups chicken broth
2 cups hot water
6 Roma tomatoes, diced
Sour cream
Cilantro

In the slow cooker, add all ingredients except for the tomatoes, cilantro, and sour cream. Mix well. Cover and cook on high for 4 to 5 hours, or on low for 7 to 8 hours. Remove bay leaves and discard. Remove chicken and shred with a fork. Return chicken to the slow cooker and mix well.

When ready to serve, spoon into individual bowls, top each with a handful of diced Roma tomatoes, a dollop of sour cream, and a few sprigs of cilantro. Serve with a side of fresh bread and a spinach salad. • Makes 6-8 Servings

Don't worry—the drowned eggs are happy eggs. They're swimming in a spicy tomato soup that's authentic and sublime.

# Drowned Egg Soup

Combine the two tomato sauces, the chicken stock, green chiles, and chicken in your slow cooker. Cover and cook on low for 4 hours.

Remove the chicken, shred with a fork, and return to the slow cooker. Drop the eggs evenly spaced throughout the soup. Pour in green enchilada sauce. Cover and cook for 30 minutes. Gently scoop the soup and one egg into each serving bowl. Serve with warm tortillas. • Makes 4 Servings

- 1 (15-ounce) can tomato sauce with garlic
- 2 (7-ounce) cans Pato® Tomato Sauce (Mexican Hot Style)
- 1 cup chicken stock
- 3 roasted green chiles, skins and seeds removed and cut into long strips
- 2 boneless chicken breasts
- 4 eggs
- 1 (15-ounce) can green enchilada sauce

Black beans are my favorite in the bean family. You'll be surprised by just how good this thick soup is. Top it off with sour cream and a squirt of lime.

# Black Bean Soup

Soak the beans overnight, and rinse them thoroughly in the morning.

In the slow cooker, mix the beans, bacon, onion, garlic, and warm chicken stock. Cover and cook on low for 8 to 9 hours.

Transfer half of the bean mixture to a blender. Purée until smooth and return to the slow cooker. Mix well. Again, transfer half of the slow cooker ingredients to a blender, purée, and return to the slow cooker. Stir in cayenne, cilantro, cumin, oregano, and sour cream. Cover and cook on low for 30 minutes. Spoon soup into individual serving bowls. Into each bowl, squeeze as much lime juice as desired. Serve with a side of salsa and tortilla chips. • Makes 4-6 Servings

- 1 pound dried black beans, sorted and rinsed
- 2 slices bacon, cut into 1/4-inch pieces
- 1 large onion, chopped
- 3 garlic cloves, chopped
- 5 cups chicken stock, warmed
- 1/2 teaspoon cayenne
- 1 tablespoon chopped cilantro
- 1 teaspoon ground cumin
- 1 teaspoon dried oregano
- 1 cup sour cream
- 3-4 limes

There are many different varieties of posole. The one thing they all have in common is hominy, which can be found in the Mexican section of almost any grocery store. What makes this version special is the red chili sauce, giving it a deep red color and rich chile flavor. If you cannot find red chile sauce, a quality enchilada sauce may be substituted.

# Red Posole

Nonstick cooking spray
1 pound lean, boneless pork, cut into 1-inch cubes
3 cups canned hominy, drained and rinsed
2 New Mexico red chiles, stemmed, seeded, and chopped
1 large onion, chopped
5 cloves garlic, crushed
1 tablespoon dried oregano
1/2 teaspoon ground cumin
5 cups chicken stock
1 1/2 cups red chile sauce
2 teaspoons salt
2 limes
4 radishes, sliced
1/2 cup cabbage, shredded
1/2 cup sour cream
Cilantro

Coat the skillet with nonstick cooking spray. Lightly brown the pork on all sides, about 4 to 5 minutes.

Combine the browned pork, hominy, chiles, onion, garlic, oregano, cumin, and chicken stock in the slow cooker. Cover and cook on low for 8 to 10 hours.

Add red chile sauce and salt. Continue cooking on low for 30 minutes or until soup is heated through. Spoon soup into serving bowls and garnish each with the juice of half a lime, radishes, cabbage, a dollop of sour cream, and cilantro. • Makes 4-6 Servings

This is one variation of a classic posole. When I used to make posole on the stovetop, I was stuck in the kitchen all afternoon. It had to be a weekend meal. Posole in the slow cooker is just as good and can be enjoyed any day of the week. Don't forget the many garnishes. They're part of what make posole something special.

# Posole Blanco

1 tablespoon olive oil
1 1/2 cups plus 1/2 cup chopped onion
1 pound lean, boneless pork, chopped into bite-size cubes
2 boneless chicken breasts, chopped into bite-size cubes
3 cloves garlic, crushed
2 (30-ounce) cans hominy
1 tablespoon dried oregano
4 cups chicken stock
1/2 teaspoon salt
4 limes, halved
2 radishes, thinly sliced
Sour cream
1 cup chopped cabbage

Heat the oil in a skillet. Add 1 1/2 cups of the onion, the pork, chicken, and garlic. Cook until the meat is browned, about 10 minutes. Combine the hominy, oregano, and chicken stock in your slow cooker and stir. Cover and cook on low for 6 to 7 hours. One hour before serving, add the salt and the remaining 1/2 cup of onion. Stir. When the soup is hot, dish into individual serving bowls, squeeze juice from half a lime into each bowl, and garnish with radishes, sour cream, and cabbage. Serve with warm tortillas. • Makes 4-6 Servings

*Albóndigas* are meatballs. They cook to perfection in this traditional Mexican soup, along with zucchini and other fresh vegetables.

# Sopa de Albóndigas

To prepare the soup, lightly sauté the onions and garlic in the oil. Combine with remaining soup ingredients in the slow cooker. Stir and turn the heat to low to begin preheating the soup while making the meatballs.

To make the meatballs, combine all meatball ingredients in a medium bowl. Mix together using your hands. Roll mixture into 1-inch meatballs, making approximately 12 to 15. Drop each meatball into the soup in the slow cooker. Cover and cook for 6 to 7 hours. Spoon into individual serving bowls, making sure each one has a few meatballs. Serve immediately.

● Makes 4-6 Servings

**Soup:**
1 medium onion, chopped
4 cloves garlic, crushed
1 teaspoon olive oil
1 (10-ounce) can diced tomatoes in sauce
1 cup can beef broth
1 medium zucchini, cut in half and then lengthwise into 1-inch slivers
2 carrots, cut into rounds
2 roasted green chiles, chopped
1/2 teaspoon ground cumin
1 teaspoon dried oregano
2 cups water
Juice of 2 limes

**Meatballs:**
1 pound ground beef
1 egg
1/2 cup onion, finely chopped
1 teaspoon garlic powder
1 teaspoon dried oregano
1/4 cup bread crumbs
1/4 teaspoon ground cumin
1/4 teaspoon salt
1/4 teaspoon pepper

We first made this delicious soup at cooking school in Mexico. Poblano chiles have a unique, rich flavor that cannot be found in other chiles, which is why they are a favorite to many people in central Mexico. The original recipe called for roasted poblanos, which can take quite some time to prepare, but by making this recipe in the slow cooker, the skins of the chiles soften enough that you don't need to remove them, and they help the soup retain its rich green color.

# Crema de Chile Poblano

Mix the potatoes, chiles, onions, garlic, dill, and water in the slow cooker. Cover and cook on low for 6 to 8 hours, or until the potatoes are tender. About 30 minutes before serving, remove the potatoes and the chiles from the slow cooker with a slotted spoon, and place in a blender. Discard the remaining ingredients from the slow cooker and rinse out. Add the milk and the sour cream to the blender with the potatoes and chiles. Blend until smooth or to the desired consistency. Return the mixture to the slow cooker, add the chicken stock, cover, and continue to cook on high for another 30 minutes, or until the soup is hot. Spoon into individual bowls, sprinkle each with a little crumbled cotija and fresh sprigs of dill, and serve with fresh, hot bread.
• Makes 6-8 Servings

2 large potatoes, peeled and cut into
    approximately 8 pieces
5 large poblano chiles, seeded and cut
    into 1-inch strips
1/2 yellow onion, coarsely chopped
4 cloves garlic, chopped
1 tablespoon dried dill
1 cup water
1 cup non-fat milk
3 tablespoons sour cream
3 cups chicken stock
1/2 cup crumbled cotija cheese
Approximately 12 sprigs fresh dill

This is a wonderful soup to serve in the fall months, when sweet potatoes are easy to find. The warmth of the chipotle and the yellow hues of the potatoes and the tomatoes give each bowl a comforting feel. If you are short on time, it will help to cut, or grate, the potatoes as finely as possible. They take a long time to soften, so the smaller the pieces, the quicker they will cook.

# Sweet Potato & Chipotle Soup

Nonstick cooking spray
2 large sweet potatoes, peeled and finely chopped
1 medium yellow onion, chopped
3 cloves garlic, chopped
2 green chiles, chopped
1 teaspoon dried rosemary
1/2 teaspoon chipotle powder
1 teaspoon salt
1/2 teaspoon black pepper
6 cups chicken broth
3 Roma tomatoes, chopped
Sour cream
12-16 sprigs cilantro

Spray the inside of the slow cooker with nonstick cooking spray. Add the sweet potatoes, onion, garlic, green chiles, rosemary, chipotle, salt, pepper, and chicken broth. Mix well. Cover and cook on low for 6 to 8 hours, or until the potatoes are very tender.

Remove approximately one-fourth of the soup from the slow cooker and place in a blender. Add one-third of the chopped tomatoes and blend until smooth. Pour into a separate bowl, and repeat with remaining soup in the slow cooker, each time adding another third of the chopped tomatoes. When finished blending, return the soup to the slow cooker, and cook for 15 to 20 more minutes, or until warmed through. To serve, spoon soup into individual bowls, add a dollop of sour cream, and garnish with a few sprigs of cilantro. Serve immediately. • Makes 6-8 Servings

Piñon trees cover northern Arizona. In the fall, when the cones are ripe, there is a great harvest of the nuts, a true delicacy. This soup is quite rich, and should be served in small bowls.

# Piñon Soup

Lightly toast the pine nuts in a skillet until slightly brown, stirring constantly so they don't burn. Transfer to the slow cooker and add chicken stock, 1 cup of the green onions, cumin, and mint leaves. Cover and cook on low 4 to 5 hours. Transfer to a blender, add milk, and blend until smooth. Top each serving with the remaining green onions. • Makes 4-6 Servings

2 cups pine nuts
1 1/2 cups chicken stock
1 cup plus 1/2 cup chopped green onions
1/2 teaspoon ground cumin
3 fresh mint leaves
1 cup milk

I created this soup the day after we had a Fourth of July barbecue. We had some leftover bratwurst, so I threw a few into the soup. We were pleasantly surprised with the hearty results! Because it is so rich and warm, I have added this soup to my must-make winter dinners.

# Spicy Sausage Soup

In a medium-sized pot, boil the sausages until cooked through, about 10 to 15 minutes. Add all ingredients except for the cilantro to the slow cooker. Stir until all of the ingredients are mixed well. Cover and cook on low for 6 to 8 hours. Approximately 30 minutes before serving, remove the sausage from the slow cooker and cut into 1/4-inch slices. Return to the slow cooker, cover, and continue cooking until warm. Spoon into individual bowls and garnish, if desired, with cilantro. • Makes 4-6 Servings

3 spicy bratwurst or hot Italian sausages
1 yellow onion, sliced
5 cloves garlic, chopped
3 green chiles, roasted and chopped
2 chipotle chiles in adobo sauce, seeded and chopped
2 tomatillos, cut into quarters
1 large tomato, chopped
1 tablespoon dried oregano
1/2 teaspoon paprika
2 (15-ounce) cans garbanzo beans, drained and rinsed
3 cups chicken stock
Cilantro

This is our very own version of a classic soup. The bread expands in the slow cooker and soaks up all of the flavors of the beef broth and onions. Day-old or hard bread is much preferred. If you only have a fresh baguette, cut it into cubes and let it sit out for a few hours before putting it in the soup.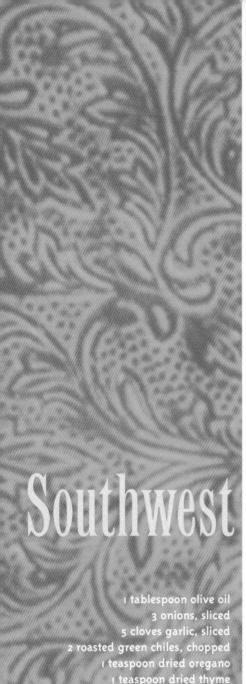

# Southwest Onion Soup

1 tablespoon olive oil
3 onions, sliced
5 cloves garlic, sliced
2 roasted green chiles, chopped
1 teaspoon dried oregano
1 teaspoon dried thyme
1 sprig fresh rosemary, leaves removed and chopped
1 (14-ounce) can diced tomatoes, undrained
1 cup of 1-inch baguette cubes
4 cups beef stock
2 limes
8 ounces queso quesadilla, thinly sliced
Cayenne

Heat the oil in a skillet. Sauté two-thirds of the onions and the garlic over low heat for 10 minutes. Combine all ingredients, except for the remaining onion, limes, cheese, and cayenne in the slow cooker. Cover and cook on low for 5 to 6 hours. Add the remaining one-third of the onion to the soup, cover, and continue to cook for 30 minutes.

Ladle soup into individual serving bowls and garnish each with lime juice. Place cheese slices over the soup and microwave for 30 seconds, or until the cheese is melted. Garnish each bowl with a dash of cayenne. • Makes 2-4 Servings

What a perfect pairing—green chiles and garbanzo beans! These two tastes of the Southwest bring out the best in this thick, authentic stew.

# Green Chile & Garbanzo Bean Stew

Dredge stewing beef in the flour and set aside. In a medium-sized frying pan, add the oil and lightly brown the onion, garlic, jalapeño, and serrano. After approximately 2 minutes, add the meat and continue to cook until the meat is lightly browned on all sides. In the slow cooker, add the browned meat mixture and all the remaining ingredients except for the basil. Stir well, cover, and cook over low heat for 6 to 8 hours. Spoon into individual serving bowls and garnish each with fresh basil. • Makes 6–8 Servings

2 pounds top round stewing beef, cut into 1-inch cubes
1/2 cup all-purpose flour
2 tablespoons olive oil
1 medium red onion, chopped
4 cloves garlic, chopped
1 jalapeño, seeded and chopped
1 serrano, seeded and chopped
2 (15-ounce) cans garbanzo beans, rinsed
2 cups beef stock, warmed
6 slices bacon, cooked and crumbled
2 green chiles, roasted and chopped
2 large tomatoes, chopped
1 teaspoon ground cumin
1 teaspoon oregano
1 teaspoon salt
1/2 teaspoon freshly ground black pepper
1 cup shredded sharp Cheddar cheese
Fresh basil

This rich stew is a Southwest classic. One of my favorite times of the year is New Mexico chile season. Our local farmers market roasts fresh chiles out in the parking lot, and there is always a line of people waiting with two, three, or even four bags full of chiles.

Some people get confused by the name of this dish. Even though it is called "chile" verde, it isn't really a "chili," meaning a thick, meaty stew. The "chile" spelling just indicates that a kind of chile pepper is being used. This dish is actually more like a thick soup or stew than a chili.

# Chile Verde

1 tablespoon vegetable oil
1 large onion, chopped
2 pounds lean, boneless pork, cut into
½-inch cubes
3 tablespoons all-purpose flour
1 teaspoon ground cumin
3 cloves garlic, crushed
15 green chiles, roasted, peeled, seeded, and chopped
1 teaspoon salt
1½ cups chicken stock
Sour cream

Heat the oil in a skillet and sauté the onions over medium heat until lightly browned, about 4 to 5 minutes. Add the pork to the onions and cook until meat is no longer pink. Slowly add the flour to the pork and onions, stir, and cook until meat is browned. Add the meat mixture to the slow cooker with the cumin, garlic, chiles, salt, and chicken stock. Stir, cover, and cook on low for 5 to 6 hours.

If the Chile Verde is not to desired thickness, in a separate bowl stir together two tablespoons of flour and two tablespoons of cold water, and add the mixture to the stew. Stir and let cook for 30 minutes. Repeat if necessary. Top with sour cream and serve with warm tortillas. ● Makes 6-8 Servings

## Potato Chile Stew

This stew is thick and hearty—the perfect remedy to a cold winter night.

1 tablespoon butter or margarine
1 pound beef stew meat, cut into 1-inch cubes
2 tablespoons all-purpose flour
1 large onion, chopped
2 cups roasted green chiles, seeds removed and chopped
2 (10-ounce) cans diced Mexican-style tomatoes, undrained
2 cloves garlic, minced
1 teaspoon ground cumin
1 large potato, peeled and cut into 1/2-inch cubes

Melt the butter in a skillet and add the beef. Sprinkle with flour and stir until meat is browned, about 5 minutes. Mix all ingredients except the potatoes in the skillet. Place the potatoes in the bottom of the slow cooker and cover with beef and chile mixture. Cover and cook on low for 8 to 10 hours. Stir and serve with sour cream and tortillas. • Makes 4-6 Servings

## Red Chile Beef Stew

If you can find fresh epazote in your market, we highly recommend that you use it. It provides a uniquely fresh taste to any dish it's added to. In a pinch, however, it can be substituted with dill or left out all together. If you can find it, you've found something special.

1 pound stewing beef, cut into 1-inch cubes
1 medium onion, chopped
3 cloves garlic, crushed
1 (15-ounce) can diced tomatoes, undrained
1 (32-ounce) can red chile sauce
3 green chiles, roasted, peeled, seeded, and chopped
1 large potato, peeled and cut into 1-inch squares
1 cup green beans
1 zucchini, cut lengthwise into 1-inch pieces
1 tablespoon dried oregano
2 epazote leaves, chopped (optional)
Cilantro

Combine all ingredients except cilantro in the slow cooker. Cover and cook on low for 7 to 9 hours. Spoon soup into individual serving bowls, and garnish each with cilantro.
• Makes 4-6 Servings

This is one of my favorite meals during the winter. Every time I'm not looking, my husband sneaks in and adds more spice. Add whatever you feel is right for you and your family. With all of the fresh vegetables mixed in, it's a very healthy, very hearty meal.

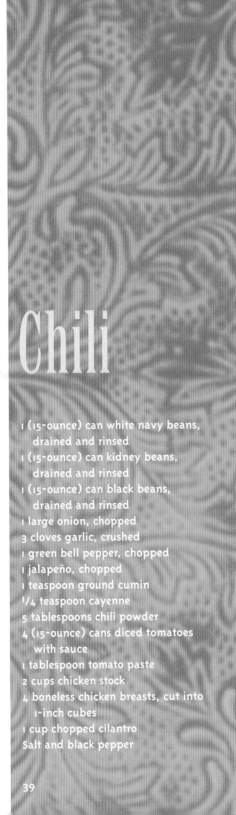

# Chicken Chili

Mix all of the ingredients except for the cilantro, salt, and pepper in your slow cooker. Cover and cook on low for 7 to 8 hours. Just before serving stir in the cilantro, and the salt and pepper to taste. Serve in individual bowls. • Makes 6-8 Servings

1 (15-ounce) can white navy beans, drained and rinsed
1 (15-ounce) can kidney beans, drained and rinsed
1 (15-ounce) can black beans, drained and rinsed
1 large onion, chopped
3 cloves garlic, crushed
1 green bell pepper, chopped
1 jalapeño, chopped
1 teaspoon ground cumin
1/4 teaspoon cayenne
5 tablespoons chili powder
4 (15-ounce) cans diced tomatoes with sauce
1 tablespoon tomato paste
2 cups chicken stock
4 boneless chicken breasts, cut into 1-inch cubes
1 cup chopped cilantro
Salt and black pepper

This delicious chili pays homage to the colors of the Mexican flag: red, white, and green. It is a wonderful blend of fresh vegetables, lightly shredded chicken, and white beans.

# Mexican Flag Chili

Add the jalapeños, onions, garlic, and beans to the slow cooker. Place chicken breasts on top of the bean mixture and sprinkle basil and cayenne over the chicken. Cover and cook on low heat for 6 to 8 hours. Fifteen minutes before serving, remove the chicken and shred with a fork. Add the shredded chicken, tomatoes, and pepper jack cheese to the slow cooker, stirring until well blended. Cover and let cook on low heat until cheese is completely melted, about 15 minutes. Spoon the chili into individual serving bowls, garnish each with cilantro, and serve with tortilla chips. • Makes 4-6 Servings

2 jalapeños, seeded and chopped
2 small white onions, chopped
5 cloves garlic, finely chopped
2 (15-ounce) cans Great Northern beans, drained and rinsed
2 boneless chicken breasts
2 tablespoons dried basil
1 teaspoon cayenne
2 Roma tomatoes, chopped
2 cups shredded pepper jack cheese
Cilantro

This is a simple vegetarian soup with a lot of flair. Throw everything into the slow cooker, turn it on, and come home to the warm, rich smells of chiles, cumin, and cayenne. Serve this hearty chili with the same kind of beer you used in the recipe, and the cold, crisp taste will bring out the best of the steaming chili.

# Three Bean Vegetarian Chili

1 red bell pepper, cut into ¼-inch strips
1 green bell pepper, cut into ¼-inch strips
5 green chiles, roasted and cut into ¼-inch strips
6 cloves garlic, chopped
1 yellow onion, chopped
1 red onion, chopped
1 (15-ounce) can black beans, drained and rinsed
1 (15-ounce) can Great Northern beans, drained and rinsed
1 (15-ounce) can pinto beans, drained and rinsed
1 tablespoon dried oregano
1 tablespoon ground cumin
1 teaspoon cayenne
1 cup light beer
1 (8-ounce) can tomato paste
Sour cream
Cilantro

Combine all ingredients except for the sour cream and cilantro in the slow cooker. Cover and cook on low for 5 to 6 hours. Spoon the chili into individual bowls and add a tablespoon of sour cream to each bowl. Stir until well blended. Garnish each bowl with fresh cilantro and serve with a side of fresh bread.
• Makes 6-8 Servings

The slow cooker perfectly complements chicken and turkey—they are not only healthy, but they are incredibly versatile. Poultry works well with a variety of ingredients, soaking up the flavors of everything it is paired with from chiles to tequila to rosemary. It's a match made in heaven!

# Poultry Entrées

Pollo y Pavo

This recipe allows you to prepare a meal that includes the meat and vegetable all in one. It calls for three large red bell peppers, but you may be able to fit four medium peppers in your slow cooker. Before you start assembling the recipe, make sure that however many peppers you have will fit into the slow cooker. If it all fits, then start cooking.

# Southwest Turkey Stuffed Peppers

1/2 pound ground turkey
1 medium onion, finely chopped
3/4 cup frozen corn kernels
1 cup bread crumbs
1 tablespoon cornmeal
1/8 tablespoon hot sauce
1/4 teaspoon salt
1/4 teaspoon pepper
1 teaspoon dried oregano
3/4 cup salsa
2 cloves garlic, crushed
3 large red bell peppers, tops cut off and seeded
1/2 cup shredded Cheddar cheese
Salsa
Sour Cream

In a large bowl, combine all ingredients except the peppers and cheese. Fill each red pepper with turkey mixture. Wrap the stuffed peppers with aluminum foil, leaving the top open, and arrange on the bottom of your slow cooker. Cover and cook on low for 5 to 6 hours. When peppers are tender, top with cheese. Turn slow cooker to high and cook until cheese is melted. Unwrap peppers, top with salsa and sour cream, and serve warm with a side of rice. • Makes 3 Servings

Yes, it involves a lot of ingredients. It's not just one of those quick "throw-it-in-the-pot" recipes, but good mole was never known for being quick.

# Turkey Mole

In a medium-sized bowl, combine sesame seeds, cilantro, cinnamon, salt, cloves, brown sugar, cumin, cayenne, oregano, cornmeal, and cocoa. Set aside. Brown turkey breasts in oil for 3 to 4 minutes or until meat is no longer pink. Coat each breast with dried mixture. Put turkey in the slow cooker and top with remaining dried mixture. Add onions, garlic, tomatoes, chipotles, raisins, and stock. Mix in ancho chiles, making sure they are covered with liquid. Top with cashews. Cover and cook on low for 7 to 8 hours.

Remove turkey breasts, shred with a fork, and set aside. Transfer the remaining ingredients to a blender and purée mole sauce until smooth. If the sauce is too thick, slowly add more water until desired thickness is reached. Return shredded turkey and sauce to the slow cooker. Cover and cook on high until the mole is heated through. Spoon turkey mole onto individual plates, top with a few sprigs of cilantro, and serve with rice and tortillas. • Makes 3-4 Servings

¹/₄ cup sesame seeds, lightly toasted
2 tablespoons chopped fresh cilantro
¹/₄ teaspoon ground cinnamon
¹/₂ teaspoon salt
¹/₈ teaspoon ground cloves
1 tablespoon brown sugar
1 teaspoon ground cumin
¹/₂ teaspoon cayenne
1 teaspoon dried oregano
2 tablespoons cornmeal
3 tablespoons cocoa
1 pound boneless turkey breast
1 tablespoon vegetable oil
1 onion, chopped
4 cloves garlic, crushed
1 (10-ounce) can puréed tomatoes
2 chipotle chiles in adobo sauce, seeded
2 tablespoons raisins
1 cup chicken stock
5 ancho chiles, seeded, stemmed,
  and chopped
¹/₄ cup cashews, toasted and chopped
Fresh cilantro

This meal is the ultimate comfort food. Try it, and you'll see why nothing else needs to be said about this warm, tasty dish.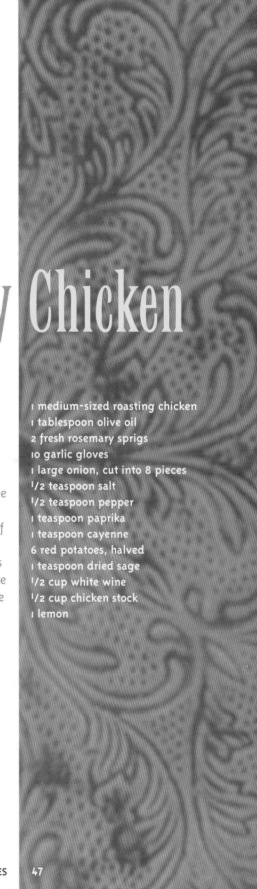

# Rosemary Chicken

Rinse the chicken in cold water. Heat oil in a skillet and lightly brown the chicken on all sides. Stuff the chicken with 1 rosemary sprig, 4 cloves of garlic, and half of the onion. Tie the legs together. Sprinkle chicken with salt, pepper, paprika, and cayenne. Set aside.

Place the potatoes, sage, the remaining onion, and garlic in the bottom of the slow cooker. Add the remaining sprig of rosemary and stir in the wine and chicken stock. Place the chicken on top of the potatoes. Squeeze the juice of one lemon over the chicken. Cover and cook on low for 8 to 9 hours. When chicken and potatoes are cooked through, remove from the slow cooker and discard the rosemary sprig from inside the chicken. Drizzle the juices over the chicken and serve. • Makes 3-4 Servings

1 medium-sized roasting chicken
1 tablespoon olive oil
2 fresh rosemary sprigs
10 garlic gloves
1 large onion, cut into 8 pieces
1/2 teaspoon salt
1/2 teaspoon pepper
1 teaspoon paprika
1 teaspoon cayenne
6 red potatoes, halved
1 teaspoon dried sage
1/2 cup white wine
1/2 cup chicken stock
1 lemon

This is a great recipe with an intense Southwest flavor. If you're serving this to your whole family, don't worry about the alcohol. The tequila adds a unique taste, and the alcohol will burn off while cooking.

# Tequila Chicken

1 tablespoon olive oil
1 tablespoon honey
3/4 cup margarita mix
1/4 cup tequila
1 tablespoon dried basil
1 teaspoon cayenne
1 teaspoon ground cumin
3-4 boneless chicken breasts
1 tablespoon all-purpose flour
1 tablespoon water
Lime wedges

In a small bowl, combine olive oil, honey, margarita mix, tequila, basil, cayenne, and cumin until well blended. Fork holes in the chicken and put in the slow cooker. Top with the olive oil mixture. Cover and cook on low heat for 5 to 6 hours.

When the chicken is cooked, remove and keep warm in an oven set at 200° F. In a separate bowl, mix the flour and water until well blended. Stir into the liquid in the slow cooker. Turn heat to high, and cook, uncovered, for 10 minutes, until the liquid thickens. Add more flour and water if a thicker sauce is desired.

Remove the chicken from the oven and cover generously with the sauce. Serve over Spanish rice with lime wedges on the side.
• Makes 3-4 Servings

This dish is delightfully simple. The only thing you really have to watch out for is that you don't overcook the rice. So if you've planned to eat dinner at 6 o'clock, be home at 6 o'clock. It's as simple as that.

# Southwest Chicken & Rice

Mix all ingredients except for the black pepper and cheese in your slow cooker. Cover and cook on low for 4 to 4 1/2 hours. Stir in pepper and top with cheese. Serve immediately.
• Makes 4–5 Servings

- 2 cups converted white rice
- 2 (10-ounce) cans diced tomatoes with sauce
- 1 (10-ounce) can diced tomatoes without sauce
- 1 tablespoon tomato paste
- 1 package taco seasoning
- 3 skinless, boneless chicken breasts, chopped into bite-sized pieces
- 1 cup corn niblets
- 1 large onion, chopped
- 1 green bell pepper, chopped
- 1/2 cup chopped roasted green chile
- 1 tablespoon garlic powder
- 1 teaspoon black pepper
- 1 cup shredded Cheddar cheese

These tortilla wraps are great for lunch or dinner. Use a good barbecue sauce that you and your family enjoy. The secret is the smooth and creamy avocado that tops it all off.

# Barbecue Chicken Tortilla Wraps

4 boneless chicken breasts
2 cups of your favorite barbecue sauce
6 (12-inch) flour tortillas
1 cup shredded Monterey jack cheese
1 avocado, peeled, seeded, and sliced
Fresh cilantro

Place the chicken breasts in the slow cooker and cover with barbecue sauce. Cover and cook on low for 5 to 6 hours. Remove chicken and shred with a fork. In the center of a warm tortilla, layer shredded chicken, cheese, avocado, and a pinch of cilantro. Roll up and enjoy! • Makes 4-6 Servings

This version of the sloppy Joe is still sloppy, but it adds a unique Southwest twist—chipotle! Once you've experienced the rich smoky flavor that the chipotle offers this dish, plain old sloppy Joes will be a thing of the past.

# Spicy Chicken Joes

2-3 boneless chicken breasts
2 yellow onions, chopped
4-5 cloves garlic, chopped
1 tablespoon olive oil
1 (8-ounce) can tomato paste
1 (16-ounce) can tomato sauce
2 chipotles in adobo sauce, seeded and chopped
1 tablespoon Worcestershire sauce
1 teaspoon ground cumin
1/2 cup packed brown sugar
1/2 teaspoon seasoning salt
4 sourdough rolls
Fresh cilantro

Lightly brown the chicken, onion, and garlic in the olive oil. In a medium-sized bowl, mix the remaining ingredients, except for the cilantro. Place the chicken mixture in the slow cooker and top with the sauce. Cover and cook on low for 5 to 6 hours, or until the chicken is cooked through.

Remove chicken and shred with a fork. Open each sourdough roll and place on individual plates. Divide the shredded chicken equally over the 4 open rolls. Top with sauce and, if desired, garnish with cilantro. • Makes 4 Servings

If you are in the mood for a meal with Southwest flair, but don't feel like taking the time to roll, shred, and bake, try this Green Chile Chicken. Throw everything in the slow cooker, turn it on, and forget about it until dinnertime.

# Green Chile Chicken

Spray the inside of the slow cooker with vegetable oil cooking spray so that the soup will not stick. Place the chicken at the bottom of the slow cooker. Add the chopped green chiles and garlic. Pour the soup over the top. Cover and cook on low for 5 to 6 hours.

Carefully remove the chicken breasts from the slow cooker and place in a 200° F. oven to keep warm. Remove the remaining sauce from the slow cooker and place in a blender. Blend until mostly smooth. Return the sauce to the slow cooker for 15 minutes. When ready to serve, place the chicken on individual serving plates, add a side of rice, and ladle the soup sauce over the top of both. Place slices of Roma tomato and avocado around the outside edge of the plate. Garnish with parsley and serve with a side of fresh cornbread. • Makes 2-3 Servings

2-3 boneless, skinless chicken breasts
3-4 green chiles, roasted, peeled, and chopped
1 (16-ounce) can cream of potato soup
3 cloves garlic, chopped
2-3 Roma tomatoes, sliced
1 ripe avocado, sliced
Fresh parsley

This satisfying meal combines the smoky flavor of chipotles with the subtle sweetness of tomatillos and brown sugar. You really cannot go wrong with this recipe. I serve this meal in a deep plate over a bed of rice. This allows you to get away with spooning more of the flavorful sauce over it all.

# Smoky Tomatillo Chicken

Thoroughly mix all ingredients except for the chicken in your slow cooker. Add the chicken and spoon the tomatillo mixture over it. Cover and cook on low for 5 to 7 hours. Serve with warm tortillas or over rice. ● Makes 3–4 Servings

15 tomatillos, shucked and crudely chopped
1 small onion, chopped
2 chipotles in adobo sauce, chopped
3 cloves garlic, crushed
1/4 cup brown sugar
1 cup chicken stock
2 tablespoons dried oregano
4 boneless chicken breasts

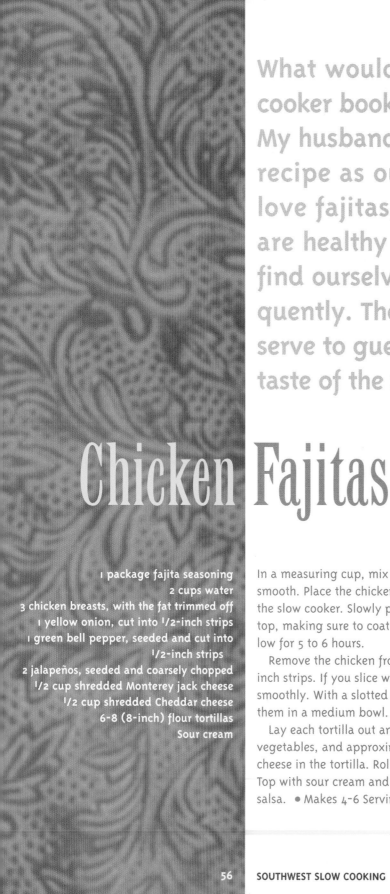

What would a Southwest slow cooker book be without fajitas? My husband and I use this tasty recipe as our standby. We love fajitas, and since they are healthy and delicious, we find ourselves eating them frequently. They are also great to serve to guests as an authentic taste of the Southwest.

# Chicken Fajitas

1 package fajita seasoning
2 cups water
3 chicken breasts, with the fat trimmed off
1 yellow onion, cut into 1/2-inch strips
1 green bell pepper, seeded and cut into 1/2-inch strips
2 jalapeños, seeded and coarsely chopped
1/2 cup shredded Monterey jack cheese
1/2 cup shredded Cheddar cheese
6-8 (8-inch) flour tortillas
Sour cream

In a measuring cup, mix the water and the fajita seasoning until smooth. Place the chicken, onion, bell pepper, and jalapeños in the slow cooker. Slowly pour the seasoned fajita water over the top, making sure to coat all of the ingredients. Cover and cook on low for 5 to 6 hours.

Remove the chicken from the slow cooker and slice into 1/2-inch strips. If you slice with the grain, the chicken will cut smoothly. With a slotted spoon, remove the vegetables and place them in a medium bowl.

Lay each tortilla out and place the chicken strips, a spoonful of vegetables, and approximately one tablespoon of shredded cheese in the tortilla. Roll and place them on individual plates. Top with sour cream and serve with a side of tortilla chips and salsa. • Makes 4-6 Servings

This dish offers an explosion of color and flavor! If you like the taste of the chipotle chiles in adobo sauce but don't like all the heat, remove the seeds and membranes from the chiles before adding them to the mixture.

# Spicy Cashew Chicken

Add all ingredients to the slow cooker, except for the cashews and cilantro. Cover and cook on low for 5 to 6 hours. When cooked, spoon the chicken mixture out of the slow cooker and serve over rice. Top with cashews and cilantro. • Makes 4-6 Servings

3 boneless chicken breasts, lightly
   browned and cut into 1/2-inch cubes
1 cup sliced jicama
1 zucchini, sliced
1 poblano chile, seeded and chopped
3 chipotle chiles in adobo sauce
1/2 cup sun-dried tomatoes
1 tablespoon dried oregano
1 cup chopped cashews
Fresh cilantro

This recipe takes two steps, but it is well worth it. In many traditional Mexican recipes, the meat needs to cook for hours, so if you don't have that much time to spend watching the stove, the slow cooker method is perfect. It is also healthier if you bake the flautas (as directed below) instead of deep-frying them.

# Flautas de Pollo

1 jalapeño, seeded and chopped
1 white onion, chopped
5 cloves garlic, finely chopped
3-4 boneless chicken breasts
1 tablespoon dried oregano
1 tablespoon black pepper
1 teaspoon chili powder
24 (6-inch) corn tortillas
1 block ranchero cheese, crumbled
Nonstick cooking spray
Corn oil

Place the jalapeño, onion, garlic, and chicken in the slow cooker. Stir in oregano, black pepper, and chili powder. Cover and cook on low for 5 to 6 hours.

Turn oven to broil. Spray a baking pan with nonstick cooking spray. Remove the chicken and vegetables from the slow cooker. Shred the chicken with a fork and mix in with the cooked vegetables. To each tortilla, add 1/2 tablespoon of the chicken mixture and 1/4 tablespoon of cheese, and then roll tightly. Put a toothpick through the center of each tortilla to hold it closed, and place on the baking pan. Repeat with remaining tortillas and mixture. When finished, brush each tortilla with a little corn oil, and place the pan in the oven for 3 to 5 minutes. Remove when tortillas are golden brown on top. Serve with a side of salsa and refried beans.
• Makes 4-6 Servings

Note: A great way to keep your tortillas from splitting when rolled is to place 3 or 4 tortillas in an unsealed plastic bag and microwave for 30 seconds. Repeat with remaining tortillas as needed. This will make them soft and pliable.

This is a simple two-step recipe. The flavors of the chicken and the vegetables infuse all day, and then they are ready to be rolled with cheese and enchilada sauce. Your whole family will ask for this meal again and again.

# Chicken & Chile Enchiladas

1 medium yellow onion, chopped
5 cloves garlic, chopped
1 poblano chile, seeded and chopped
2-3 boneless chicken breasts
2 green chiles, roasted and chopped
1 tablespoon dried oregano
1 teaspoon cayenne
1 (32-ounce) jar green enchilada sauce
Nonstick cooking spray
1 cup light sour cream
2 medium tomatoes, chopped
2 cups shredded Monterey jack cheese
12 (6-inch) corn tortillas

In the slow cooker, combine the onion, garlic, poblano, chicken, green chiles, oregano, and cayenne. Over the top, pour 1 cup of the enchilada sauce, making sure to lightly coat the chicken. Cover and cook on low for 5 to 6 hours.

Preheat oven to 350° F. and lightly coat the bottom of a 13 x 9-inch baking pan with nonstick cooking spray. Remove chicken from slow cooker and shred with a fork. Set aside. In a large bowl, combine the remaining ingredients from the slow cooker, the remaining enchilada sauce, the sour cream, and the chopped tomatoes. Stir well.

Dip one tortilla at a time in the mixture, making sure it is well coated. Add 1 tablespoon shredded chicken and 1/2 tablespoon shredded cheese to the center. Carefully roll the filled tortilla and place in the baking pan. Repeat until all tortillas are in the pan. Spread remaining enchilada mixture over the top of the tortillas and spread evenly. Sprinkle remaining cheese over the top, and cook in the oven for 20 to 30 minutes or until heated through. Serve warm with tortilla chips. • Makes 4-6 Servings

Note: A great way to keep your tortillas from splitting when rolled is to place 3 to 4 tortillas in an unsealed plastic bag and microwave for 30 seconds. Repeat with remaining tortillas as needed. This will make them soft and pliable.

Sweet and spicy flavors are beautiful accompaniments to pork. Luckily, spicy and sweet flavors are a staple of Southwest cuisine. The recipes in this chapter offer some amazing pairings, such as chipotles with raspberries, mangoes with habaneros, and many more—all served with pork.

 # Pork Entrées

## Puerco

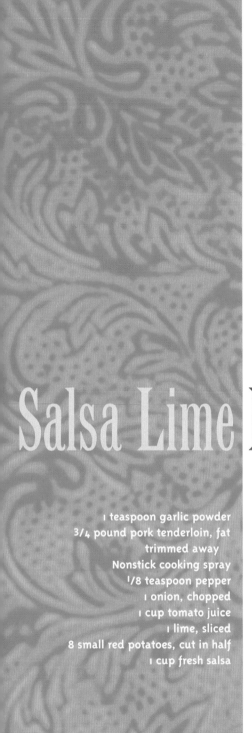

Just the name of this recipe makes us think of warm summer days in Mexico, salsa rhythms, congas, and fresh flavors. The combination of the salsa and the lime makes the tenderloin zing. Use your favorite bottled salsa—as mild or as hot as you like it.

# Salsa Lime Pork Tenderloin

1 teaspoon garlic powder
3/4 pound pork tenderloin, fat trimmed away
Nonstick cooking spray
1/8 teaspoon pepper
1 onion, chopped
1 cup tomato juice
1 lime, sliced
8 small red potatoes, cut in half
1 cup fresh salsa

Sprinkle garlic powder over pork. Lightly coat a skillet with nonstick cooking spray and brown the pork until it is no longer pink. Sprinkle with pepper, remove from skillet, and set aside. Sauté onions for 2 to 3 minutes.

Pour tomato juice into the slow cooker and place pork into the tomato juice. Cover with lime slices and sautéed onions. Arrange potatoes around the edges and pour salsa on top. Cover and cook on low for 6 to 7 hours.

When pork is cooked through and potatoes are tender, remove from the slow cooker and cut into individual portions. Place each portion on a serving plate, top with remaining sauce, and serve.

● Makes 3-4 Servings

Habaneros enjoy the fame of being the hottest chile out there. Pow! Combined with the mango and the ketchup, however, the heat is balanced with the sweet. You'll find that one habanero, finely chopped, provides just the right amount of heat.

# Mango Habanero Pork Chops

Combine all ingredients except for the pork in a medium-sized bowl. Place pork chops in the bottom of your slow cooker and cover with the mango sauce. Cover and cook on low for 6 to 7 hours. Serve over rice. • Makes 4 Servings

1 (15-ounce) can mangoes in syrup
1 small onion, chopped
1 habanero chile, finely chopped
1/2 cup ketchup
1 tablespoon brown sugar
4 lean boneless pork chops

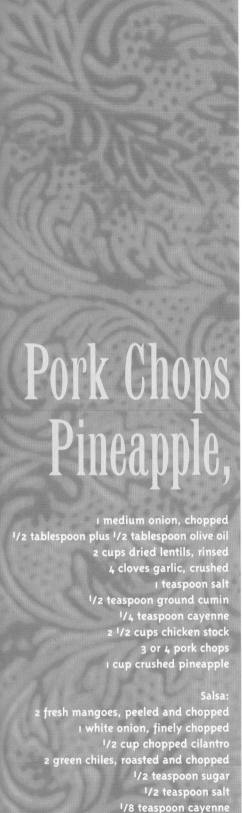

The lentils and the fruit complement the pork beautifully in this recipe. If you are unable to find fresh mangoes or just don't have the time to whip up a bowl of fresh salsa, there are some good pre-made varieties on the market.

# Pork Chops with Lentils, Pineapple, and Mango Salsa

1 medium onion, chopped
1/2 tablespoon plus 1/2 tablespoon olive oil
2 cups dried lentils, rinsed
4 cloves garlic, crushed
1 teaspoon salt
1/2 teaspoon ground cumin
1/4 teaspoon cayenne
2 1/2 cups chicken stock
3 or 4 pork chops
1 cup crushed pineapple

Salsa:
2 fresh mangoes, peeled and chopped
1 white onion, finely chopped
1/2 cup chopped cilantro
2 green chiles, roasted and chopped
1/2 teaspoon sugar
1/2 teaspoon salt
1/8 teaspoon cayenne
Juice of one lime

Sauté the onions in 1/2 tablespoon of the oil until translucent. Add the lentils, garlic, and salt, and cook over medium heat for about 5 minutes. Transfer lentil mixture to slow cooker. Add cumin, cayenne, and chicken stock.

Brown the pork chops in the remaining 1/2 tablespoon of oil over medium heat, about 7 to 8 minutes. Arrange pork chops on top of lentils in slow cooker. Cover and cook on low for 6 to 7 hours. When cooked through, remove chops and set aside. Add the crushed pineapple to the lentil mixture and stir. Return pork chops to the slow cooker, cover, and continue cooking on low while you prepare the mango salsa.

To prepare the mango salsa, mix all of the ingredients together in a medium-sized bowl.

Spread the lentils on individual plates. Place the pork chops on top and cover with mango salsa. • Makes 3-4 Servings

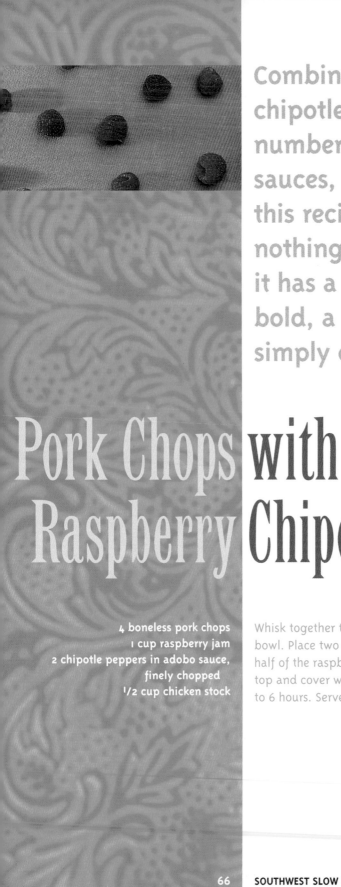

Combine raspberries and chipotles together to create a number of sweet yet spicy sauces, from salad dressing to this recipe here. There's really nothing to it, but when served it has a real gourmet feel. It's bold, a little different, but simply delicious.

# Pork Chops with Raspberry Chipotle Sauce

4 boneless pork chops
1 cup raspberry jam
2 chipotle peppers in adobo sauce, finely chopped
1/2 cup chicken stock

Whisk together the jam, chipotles, and stock in a medium-sized bowl. Place two pork chops in your slow cooker and cover with half of the raspberry sauce. Stack remaining two pork chops on top and cover with remaining sauce. Cover and cook on low for 5 to 6 hours. Serve with rice and a salad. • Makes 4 Servings

There's no doubt about it—this is a casserole, but it's one that you won't have to worry about cooking come five o'clock. With the slow cooker, it's ready when you are. This is actually an adaptation of a recipe that my mom served to us when we were kids. It's hearty, delicious, and keeps everyone happy.

# Calabacitas & Sausage

Remove sausage from casings and brown in a skillet for about 10 minutes. In the meantime, boil the whole zucchinis for 5 minutes. Remove from the water and chop. Drain the browned sausage and mix together with the remaining ingredients, except the cheese. Add to slow cooker, cover, and cook on low for 5 to 6 hours. When the vegetables are tender, remove from slow cooker, top with cheese, and serve warm. • Makes 4-5 Servings

1 pound turkey sausage
2 medium zucchinis
1/2 onion, chopped
1 clove garlic, chopped
1/2 cup frozen corn kernels
1 teaspoon dried oregano
1 teaspoon chile powder
3 slices white bread, cubed
1 cup shredded mozzarella cheese

I just love the flavor and aroma a lager beer adds to a slow cooker recipe. This is a new twist on the old pork and beans standby—perfect for a Saturday night. My husband and I make a habit of buying a six-pack of lager, adding one to the pot, and enjoying dinner with some friends and the rest of the beer.

# Spicy Pork & Beans

Combine all of the ingredients except for the cilantro and salt in the slow cooker. Cover and cook on low for 7 to 8 hours. Stir in the cilantro and salt, and serve with warm tortillas and sour cream. • Makes 4-5 Servings

1 pound lean pork, chopped into
    bite-sized pieces
1 (12-ounce) can lager beer
2 jalapeños, chopped
1 can pinto beans, drained and rinsed
1 bunch cilantro, chopped
1 teaspoon salt

This is an original barbecue recipe and it's hot, just the way we like it! You can adjust the heat by reducing the amount of chipotles you use. When you eat the barbecue as a sandwich, the cheese and the jicama will also help to balance the heat.

# Barbecue Pork

2 onions, chopped
5 cloves garlic
1 teaspoon ground cumin
1 (15-ounce) can diced tomatoes
1/2 cup molasses
1/2 cup cider vinegar
2 tablespoons tomato paste
1/4 cup packed brown sugar
1 can chipotles in adobo sauce, seeds and membranes removed
2 pounds pork rib roast
1 bay leaf
4 Kaiser rolls
1 cup shredded Cheddar cheese
1 cup finely chopped jicama

Combine the onion, garlic, cumin, diced tomatoes, molasses, vinegar, tomato paste, brown sugar, and chipotles in the blender. Purée until smooth, about 1–2 minutes. Pour mixture into slow cooker. In a skillet, lightly brown rib roast on all sides. Place in slow cooker. Add the bay leaf. Cover and cook on low for 7 to 8 hours.

Remove pork roast, shred with a fork, and return to slow cooker. Discard the bay leaf. Continue cooking on low until barbecue sauce and pork are heated through. Spoon pork mixture onto individual Kaiser rolls, sprinkle each with cheese and jicama, and serve.

• Makes 4 Servings

This dish is a fusion of flavor! The ham soaks up the subtle flavors of green chiles, onions, and chipotle, blended with the fresh sweetness of golden raisins. It is especially good when accompanied by a cold Mexican beer.

# Sweet & Spicy Ham

In a medium-sized bowl, combine tomato sauce, green chiles, onion, Worcestershire, and chipotle. Stir until well blended. In the slow cooker, layer the slices of ham, covering each piece with some of the tomato mixture. Repeat layers until all the ham is in the slow cooker. Add remaining mixture to the top and sides of the slow cooker. Cover and cook on low for 3 to 4 hours. When done, remove ham slices from the slow cooker, place on individual plates, spoon sauce over each slice, and top with a handful of shredded cheese and raisins. Serve with a side of rice. • Makes 4 Servings

1 (15-ounce) can tomato sauce
2 (4-ounce) cans chopped green chiles
1 yellow onion, chopped
1 tablespoon Worcestershire sauce
1/2 teaspoon chipotle powder
1 1/2 pounds lean, cooked ham, cut into 1/4-inch thick slices
1 cup shredded Monterey jack cheese
Golden raisins

Traditionally, carnitas are fried. This recipe offers a healthier version without sacrificing flavor. The pork in this dish is incredibly tender and full of the wonderful flavors of beer, jalapeño, and cilantro. It can be wrapped in a tortilla or served on its own.

# Carnitas

With a knife, make four small cuts on each side of the pork. Insert one garlic clove into each cut. Place the pork into the slow cooker and cover with the cilantro and jalapeño. Pour the beer over the pork. Cover and cook on high for 5 to 6 hours.

When the dish is done cooking, shred the pork with a fork in the slow cooker. Serve in warmed flour tortillas and top with sour cream and your favorite salsa. • Makes 5-6 Servings

2-3 pounds pork butt, extra fat removed
8 cloves garlic, peeled
1 bunch cilantro, chopped
1 jalapeño, seeded and chopped
1 (12-ounce) can lager beer

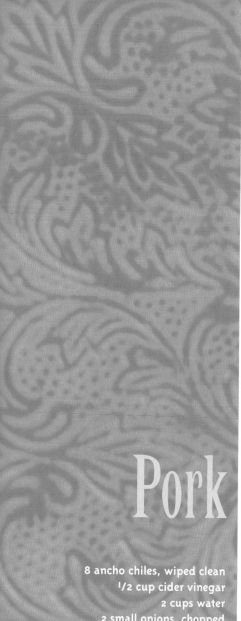

This recipe will take a little more time upfront to prepare, but the only way to make a good pork adobada is to take time in preparing the adobo sauce and then cook the pork all day long. Thank goodness for the slow cooker. Once you make the sauce, sit down and relax; a wonderfully rich dish awaits you.

# Pork Adobada

8 ancho chiles, wiped clean
1/2 cup cider vinegar
2 cups water
2 small onions, chopped
5 cloves garlic, chopped
1 tablespoon ground cumin
1 cup chicken stock
1/2 cup orange juice
2 tablespoons brown sugar
2 tablespoons tomato paste
1 tablespoon all-purpose flour
3 pounds lean pork meat, chopped into bite-sized pieces
Salt and black pepper

On a hot cast-iron skillet, toast the anchos until they begin to dance on the skillet and bubble. Be sure to turn them often so they do not burn. Transfer them to a pot and add vinegar and water. Bring to a boil and then simmer for 20 minutes.

In the meantime, toss the onion, garlic, and chicken stock into the slow cooker. In a small bowl stir together the orange juice, brown sugar, tomato paste, and flour, and add to the slow cooker.

After the anchos are sufficiently softened, transfer the chiles and one cup of the liquid to a blender. Blend until the chiles and liquid form a thick paste. Stir the paste into the slow cooker.

Add the pork and stir to ensure that all of the meat is covered with sauce. Cover and cook on low for 6 to 8 hours. Add salt and pepper to taste, and serve with warm tortillas and an assortment of your favorite fixings. • Makes 6-8 Servings

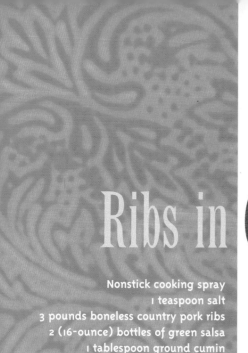

This is one of those easy, throw-it-in-the-slow cooker, expect-a-great-meal recipes. When choosing a green salsa, try to pick one with tomatillos and jalapeños. The flavors blend together especially well with the pork ribs.

# Ribs in Green Sauce

Nonstick cooking spray
1 teaspoon salt
3 pounds boneless country pork ribs
2 (16-ounce) bottles of green salsa
1 tablespoon ground cumin
1 tablespoon garlic powder

Coat a skillet with nonstick cooking spray. Season the ribs with the salt and lightly brown in the skillet, about 5 to 8 minutes. Combine the salsa, cumin, and garlic in a medium bowl. Place the browned ribs in the slow cooker and cover with the green sauce. Cover and cook on low for 8 to 9 hours. Serve with warm tortillas and sour cream. • Makes 4–5 Servings

This is my parents' favorite slow cooker recipe with a new addition—chipotle powder. The rich, smoky flavor of chipotle blends perfectly with barbecue sauce. Feel free to make your own sauce, but this recipe is just as good if you use a quality prepared barbecue sauce.

# Barbecue Spareribs

4–6 country spareribs
1 (8-ounce) bottle prepared barbecue sauce
1 teaspoon chipotle powder

Preheat the oven to 350° F. Place the spareribs on a cookie sheet and bake for approximately 20 minutes. This will help bake off some of the excess fat.

In a medium bowl, mix the barbecue sauce and the chipotle powder. Place the spare ribs in the slow cooker and cover with most of the sauce. Reserve approximately 3 to 4 tablespoons of sauce for later. Cover and cook on low for 6 to 8 hours.

Preheat the oven to 350° F. again. Remove the ribs from the slow cooker and place on the cookie sheet. Brush the ribs with the reserved sauce, and bake for 15 to 20 minutes more, so that the sauce will stick. Serve hot with a side of rice and a lot of napkins! • Makes 4–6 Servings

Close the book on that tired old pot roast and potatoes recipe. Here begins a whole new chapter on exciting beef entrées! Included are some traditional dishes with some surprising twists. In this chapter, you'll find a fusion of cultures and generations all wrapped up in a warm tortilla.

 # Beef Entrées

## Carne

South-of-the-Border Casserole
Mexican Meatloaf
Rockin' Round Roast
Southwest Beef Brisket
Bistek en Relleno
Brian's Southwest-Style Pot Roast
One-Pot Dinner
Garlic-Stuffed Beef with Chipotle
Machaca
Dave's Grilled Steak Tacos
José O'Malley's Authentic Enchiladas
Shredded Beef Soft Tacos

My husband whipped up this delicious casserole after returning from a seaside adventure in Puerto Peñasco. It infuses all of the traditional flavors of Mexico, while retaining its duty as a winter comfort food. Head south of the border and serve this flavorful casserole tonight!

# South-of-the-Border Casserole

1 pound lean ground beef
1 yellow onion, chopped
4 cloves garlic, chopped
¼ cup salsa
5 green chiles, chopped
1 (16-ounce) can corn kernels, drained
1 poblano chile, seeded and chopped
1 large tomato, chopped
1 tablespoon oregano
1 teaspoon black pepper
Nonstick cooking spray
6 (6-inch) corn tortillas, cut into 1-inch strips
2 cups shredded Colby jack cheese
Sour cream
Fresh cilantro

Brown the meat, onions, and garlic in a large frying pan. Add the salsa and cook until the meat is cooked though. Mix in the green chiles, corn, poblano chile, tomato, oregano, and pepper.

Coat the inside of the slow cooker with cooking spray. In the slow cooker, layer the tortilla strips, meat and vegetable mixture, and cheese. Repeat as necessary. You should have 2 or 3 layers depending on how thick you make each one. Cover and cook on low for 4 to 5 hours, or until heated through and cheese is melted. Allow to cool for 10 minutes, and then remove from the slow cooker with a large serving spoon. Place on individual serving plates, top with sour cream, and garnish with cilantro. ● Makes 4-6 Servings

Meatloaf doesn't have to be boring any longer! This Mexican version spices it up and adds some unexpected flavors.

# Mexican Meatloaf

Lightly coat the inside of the slow cooker with nonstick cooking spray. Mix the remaining ingredients together in a large bowl. Shape into a loaf and place on the bottom of the slow cooker. Cover and cook for 6 to 8 hours on low or until meat is no longer pink. When cooked through, cut into squares and carefully remove from the slow cooker. This meal is especially good when served with a fresh spinach salad. • Makes 6-8 Servings

Nonstick cooking spray
2 pounds lean ground beef
1/2 package taco seasoning mix
2 cups bread crumbs
2 large eggs
1 cup shredded Cheddar cheese
1 (16-ounce) can corn kernels, drained
1 medium-sized onion, chopped
1/2 cup spicy salsa

The chili sauce gives what might look, at a first glance, like a traditional pot roast a special kick. Out with the old. In with the new. Take that tired pot roast recipe and turn it into something exceptional.

# Rockin' Round Roast

Mix the flour, mustard, chili sauce, Worcestershire, vinegar, and brown sugar in a small bowl. Set aside. Place the potatoes and onion on the bottom of the slow cooker. Add the round roast, and then top with most of the mustard mixture, reserving about 3 tablespoons. Cover and cook on low for 8 to 10 hours, or until meat and vegetables are cooked through. When ready to serve, remove roast, slice, and place on individual plates. Drizzle with reserved mustard mixture. With a slotted spoon, remove remaining vegetables. Serve immediately. • Makes 6-8 Servings

2 tablespoons all-purpose flour
1 tablespoon spicy brown mustard
1 tablespoon chili sauce
1 tablespoon Worcestershire sauce
1 tablespoon red wine vinegar
2 teaspoons packed brown sugar
4 red potatoes, sliced into quarters
1 white onion, chopped
3-4 pounds round roast

Blending the juices left in your slow cooker after the meat and vegetables in this recipe have been cooking all day makes a rich and flavorful gravy.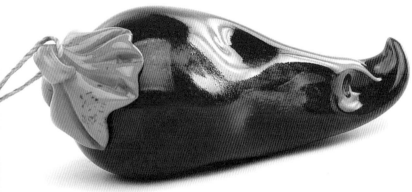

# Southwest Beef Brisket

3 pounds beef brisket
Salt and black pepper
1 tablespoon all-purpose flour
2 tablespoons vegetable oil
3 carrots, peeled and cut into 1-inch diagonal slices
2 onions, chopped
10 cloves garlic, chopped
2 chipotle peppers in adobo sauce, seeded
2 tablespoons tomato paste
1 tablespoon oregano
1/2 cup red wine vinegar
1/2 cup chicken stock
5 red potatoes, quartered
3 bay leaves

Lightly season brisket with salt and pepper. Dredge in flour. Heat oil in a skillet over high heat. Brown the meat on all sides, remove from the skillet, and set aside.

Place remaining ingredients in the slow cooker and gently stir. Place meat on top of the vegetables. Cover and cook on low for 8 to 10 hours.

With a slotted spoon, remove meat and potatoes and set aside. Discard the bay leaves. In a blender, purée remaining slow cooker ingredients until smooth. Return sauce to the slow cooker and add the meat and potatoes. Cook on high until heated through. When ready to serve, remove meat and slice. Place on individual plates with a side of the potatoes and drizzle with the sauce.

• Makes 5-6 Servings

This was one of my favorite meals from Mexican Home Cooking School in Tlaxcala, Mexico. Under Señor John's supervision, we turned ordinary beef rolls into magical Bistek en Rellenos. You can serve this bistek with the sauce recipe below, or, if you don't have the time to make it, you can use a prepared red chile sauce.

# Bistek en Relleno

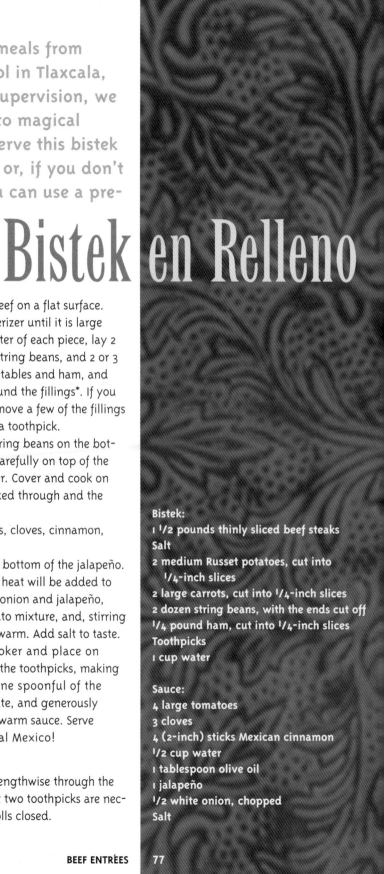

To make the beef rolls, place each piece of beef on a flat surface. Pound one piece at a time with a meat tenderizer until it is large enough to roll easily. Salt lightly. On the center of each piece, lay 2 or 3 potato slices, 2 or 3 carrot slices, 2 or 3 string beans, and 2 or 3 pieces of ham. Roll the beef around the vegetables and ham, and with a toothpick, close the beef securely around the fillings*. If you cannot close the beef around the fillings, remove a few of the fillings until you can securely close each piece with a toothpick.

Place the unused potatoes, carrots, and string beans on the bottom of the slow cooker. Layer the beef rolls carefully on top of the vegetables. Add the water to the slow cooker. Cover and cook on low for 6 to 8 hours, or until the beef is cooked through and the vegetables are tender.

To make the red sauce, blend the tomatoes, cloves, cinnamon, and water until very smooth. Set aside.

Using a sharp knife, make an "x" near the bottom of the jalapeño. (The larger you make the opening, the more heat will be added to the sauce.) In a large frying pan, brown the onion and jalapeño, about 3 to 4 minutes. Add the blended tomato mixture, and, stirring constantly, cook for 5 to 7 minutes, or until warm. Add salt to taste.

Remove the beef rolls from the slow cooker and place on individual serving plates. Carefully remove the toothpicks, making sure that the beef rolls stay closed. Add one spoonful of the vegetables from the slow cooker to each plate, and generously cover the beef rolls and vegetables with the warm sauce. Serve immediately and enjoy this taste of central Mexico!

• Makes 4-6 Servings

*Note: It works best to weave the toothpick lengthwise through the beef like a sewing needle. You may find that two toothpicks are necessary on larger pieces of beef to keep the rolls closed.

**Bistek:**
1 1/2 pounds thinly sliced beef steaks
Salt
2 medium Russet potatoes, cut into 1/4-inch slices
2 large carrots, cut into 1/4-inch slices
2 dozen string beans, with the ends cut off
1/4 pound ham, cut into 1/4-inch slices
Toothpicks
1 cup water

**Sauce:**
4 large tomatoes
3 cloves
4 (2-inch) sticks Mexican cinnamon
1/2 cup water
1 tablespoon olive oil
1 jalapeño
1/2 white onion, chopped
Salt

My husband loves cooking, especially when beef is involved. A little bit of this and a little bit of that result in this hearty pot roast. The only thing better than coming home to a home-cooked meal in the slow cooker is coming home to one prepared by your husband.

# Brian's Southwest-Style Pot Roast

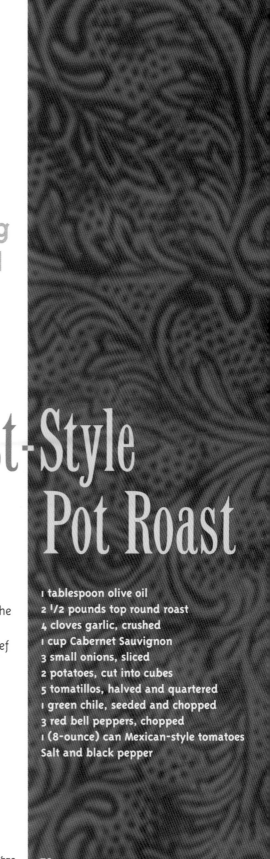

Heat the olive oil in a pan and lightly brown the beef. Set aside. Add all remaining ingredients to the slow cooker and top with the beef. Cover and cook on low for 9 to 10 hours.

When beef and vegetables are thoroughly cooked, remove beef from the slow cooker and slice to desired thickness. Remove remaining vegetables with a slotted spoon and set aside. On individual serving plates, add the sliced beef and the vegetables, and then drizzle with the sauce remaining in the slow cooker. This dish is especially good when served with a side of rice.

• Makes 4-6 Servings

1 tablespoon olive oil
2 1/2 pounds top round roast
4 cloves garlic, crushed
1 cup Cabernet Sauvignon
3 small onions, sliced
2 potatoes, cut into cubes
5 tomatillos, halved and quartered
1 green chile, seeded and chopped
3 red bell peppers, chopped
1 (8-ounce) can Mexican-style tomatoes
Salt and black pepper

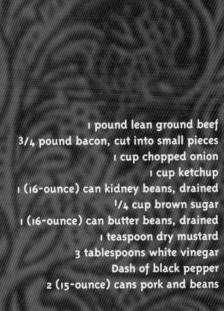

This tasty dish has everything you need for a hearty meal, and it's so easy that you're only one step away from the dinner table.

# One-Pot Dinner

1 pound lean ground beef
3/4 pound bacon, cut into small pieces
1 cup chopped onion
1 cup ketchup
1 (16-ounce) can kidney beans, drained
1/4 cup brown sugar
1 (16-ounce) can butter beans, drained
1 teaspoon dry mustard
3 tablespoons white vinegar
Dash of black pepper
2 (15-ounce) cans pork and beans

Brown the ground beef in a skillet. Drain off the fat, and put beef in the slow cooker. Brown the bacon and onion. Drain excess fat. Add the bacon, onion, and remaining ingredients to the slow cooker. Stir together well, cover, and cook on low for 4 to 6 hours. • Makes 6-8 Servings

Chipotle is an old flavor with renewed popularity. I was first introduced to the chipotle, which is a dried, smoked jalapeño, while in Mexico at cooking school. Doña Estela gave us a lesson on all of the varieties of fresh and dried chiles, and the one I was most fascinated with was the chipotle.

# Garlic-Stuffed Beef with Chipotle

1 (3-5 pound) round roast
6 cloves garlic, cut in halves
2 (10-ounce) cans diced tomatoes, undrained
2 chipotles in adobo sauce, seeded and chopped
2 tablespoons adobo sauce
Fresh cilantro

Place the round roast on a cutting board. Make 12 cuts, approximately 1 inch deep, scattered across the top of the roast. Insert half a garlic clove in each slit, making sure the garlic is pushed into the roast as far as it will go. Place the roast in the slow cooker. Add the diced tomatoes with their juice, the chopped chipotles, and the adobo sauce to the slow cooker. Cover and cook on low for 6 to 8 hours.

Remove the roast from the slow cooker and slice carefully across the grain. Place the slices of beef on a serving platter and drizzle some of the tomato-chipotle sauce from the slow cooker over the top. Garnish with a few sprigs of cilantro. Serve with a side of rosemary potatoes and a spinach salad. • Makes 4-6 Servings

Machaca—dried, shredded beef—is a traditional Mexican dish, so when we were planning this cookbook, we knew that we had to include a machaca recipe. It turns out that a friend of ours has been working on perfecting his own variation of machaca for years now, and he offered us this recipe. Thanks, Justin. It is truly delicious!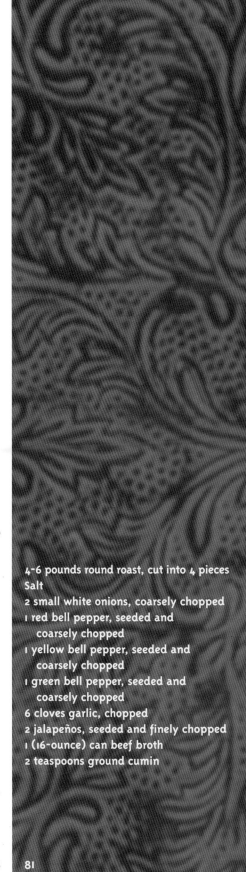

# Machaca

Lay the pieces of beef on a plate and generously salt each side of the meat. Place the salted beef in the slow cooker and add the remaining ingredients. Cover and cook on low for 4 to 5 hours. Remove all of the liquid from the slow cooker. Cover and cook on low again for another 3 to 4 hours.

Remove the beef from the slow cooker, leaving the other vegetables in the slow cooker. Coarsely shred the beef with a fork. Lightly salt the shredded beef, and return it to the slow cooker, making sure that the beef stays on the top of the vegetables. Cook on low, uncovered, for 1 hour more. This process will dry out the outside layer of the beef, while retaining the moisture inside.

After approximately 1 hour, mix the shredded beef with the vegetables in the slow cooker, and remove to a separate bowl. Use as a filling in any of your favorite dishes, such as tacos, burritos, or tostadas. The dried beef tastes especially good when accompanied by crumbled cotija or ranchero cheese. • Makes 4-6 Servings

4-6 pounds round roast, cut into 4 pieces
Salt
2 small white onions, coarsely chopped
1 red bell pepper, seeded and coarsely chopped
1 yellow bell pepper, seeded and coarsely chopped
1 green bell pepper, seeded and coarsely chopped
6 cloves garlic, chopped
2 jalapeños, seeded and finely chopped
1 (16-ounce) can beef broth
2 teaspoons ground cumin

This recipe, which has grown to be a favorite, is my husband's legacy to our slow cooker family tradition. By lightly browning the meat first, you can cut down on the cooking time, while helping to retain the meat's tasty juices. And the unexpected fusion of Southwest and Caribbean flavors is sure to make this one of your family favorites, too.

# Dave's Grilled Steak Tacos

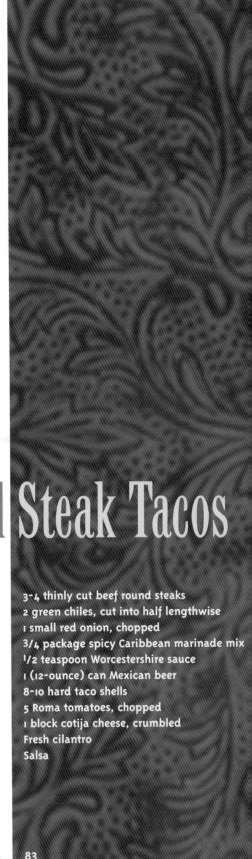

Grill the steaks until slightly browned, about 5 to 7 minutes. Cut them into strips and put in the slow cooker with the green chiles, onion, marinade mix, Worcestershire, and beer. Cover and cook on low for 3 to 4 hours. When beef is cooked through, remove with a slotted spoon and set aside. In each taco shell, add approximately 1 tablespoon of the beef, 1 tablespoon tomatoes, and 1 tablespoon cheese. Top with cilantro. Repeat until all taco shells have been filled. Serve with your favorite salsa.

• Makes 3-4 Servings

3-4 thinly cut beef round steaks
2 green chiles, cut into half lengthwise
1 small red onion, chopped
3/4 package spicy Caribbean marinade mix
1/2 teaspoon Worcestershire sauce
1 (12-ounce) can Mexican beer
8-10 hard taco shells
5 Roma tomatoes, chopped
1 block cotija cheese, crumbled
Fresh cilantro
Salsa

So many traditional Mexican dishes take hours on the stovetop to cook. Now you can just throw your ingredients in the slow cooker and let the flavors infuse all day. This easy two-step dish adds the unexpected taste of corned beef that takes this recipe to a new culinary level.

# José O'Malley's Authentic Enchiladas

1 red onion, chopped
1 habanero, seeded and chopped
2 serranos, seeded and chopped
4 cloves garlic, finely chopped
1 corned beef brisket, fat trimmed off and cut into 4 quarters
1 (32-ounce) can red enchilada sauce
Nonstick cooking spray
1 tablespoon dried oregano
12 (6-inch) white corn tortillas
1 block panela cheese, cut into thin strips
1 block ranchero cheese, crumbled
1 avocado, coarsely chopped
6-8 sprigs fresh oregano

Place the onion, habanero, serranos, garlic, and brisket in the slow cooker. Top with approximately 4 tablespoons of the enchilada sauce. Cover and cook on low for 7 to 8 hours, or until meat and vegetables are thoroughly cooked.

Preheat the oven to 350° F. Coat a 13 x 9-inch baking pan with cooking spray and set aside. Remove the beef from the slow cooker and shred it with a fork. Set aside. Pour the enchilada sauce with the vegetables into a large mixing bowl. Add the remaining enchilada sauce and oregano and mix well.

Dip one tortilla at a time in the enchilada mixture, making sure it is well coated. Add approximately 1 tablespoon of the shredded beef and 2 or 3 strips of the panela cheese to the center. Carefully roll the filled tortilla and place in the baking pan. Repeat with remaining tortillas, beef, and cheese until the pan is full. Pour approximately 3 tablespoons of the enchilada mixture over each enchilada. Sprinkle ranchero cheese over the top, and cook in the oven for 25 to 30 minutes, or until heated through.

When ready to serve, place 1 or 2 enchiladas on each plate, spoon a little warm enchilada sauce over the top, and top with chopped avocado and a sprig of fresh oregano. • Makes 6-8 Servings

Note: A great way to keep your tortillas from splitting when rolled is to place 3 or 4 tortillas in an unsealed plastic bag and microwave for 30 seconds. Repeat with remaining tortillas as needed. This will make them soft and pliable.

These are not your ordinary shredded beef tacos. By adding the crumbly richness of ranchero cheese, you will be discovering a whole new way to bring tacos to life.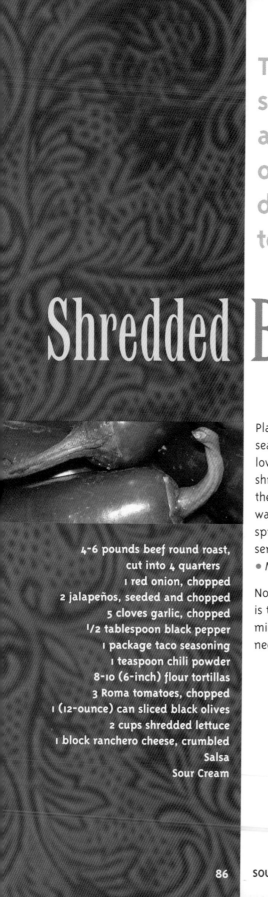

# Shredded Beef Soft Tacos

4-6 pounds beef round roast,
cut into 4 quarters
1 red onion, chopped
2 jalapeños, seeded and chopped
5 cloves garlic, chopped
1/2 tablespoon black pepper
1 package taco seasoning
1 teaspoon chili powder
8-10 (6-inch) flour tortillas
3 Roma tomatoes, chopped
1 (12-ounce) can sliced black olives
2 cups shredded lettuce
1 block ranchero cheese, crumbled
Salsa
Sour Cream

Place the round roast, onion, jalapeños, garlic, black pepper, taco seasoning, and chili powder in the slow cooker. Cover and cook on low for 6 to 8 hours. With a slotted spoon, remove the beef and shred it with a fork. Set aside. Remove remaining ingredients from the slow cooker and add to the shredded beef. Mix well. To each warmed tortilla, add 1 tablespoon of the meat mixture, and then sprinkle with tomato, black olives, lettuce, and cheese. Roll and serve immediately with your favorite salsa and sour cream.
• Makes 6-8 Servings

Note: A great way to keep your tortillas from splitting when rolled is to place 3 or 4 tortillas in an unsealed plastic bag and microwave for 30 seconds. Repeat with remaining tortillas as needed. This will make them soft and pliable.

The challenge in preparing any good vegetarian meal is finding a way to combine well-balanced healthy ingredients without sacrificing flavor. These recipes are delicious, satisfying, nutritious, and a true taste of the Southwest.

# Vegetarian Entrées Vegetariano

**Vegetarian Stuffed Peppers**
**Stuffed Onions with Cheese Sauce**
**Paella Roja**
**Potato Burritos**
**Spinach & Potato Pancakes**
**Chile Relleno Casserole**
**Corn Bread Casserole**
**Southwest Quiche**

Some people shy away from cooking rice in their slow cooker. Converted rice (such as Uncle Ben's®), however, works beautifully. Just make sure not to overcook this one. Come dinner time, you'll have a satisfying vegetarian meal waiting for you.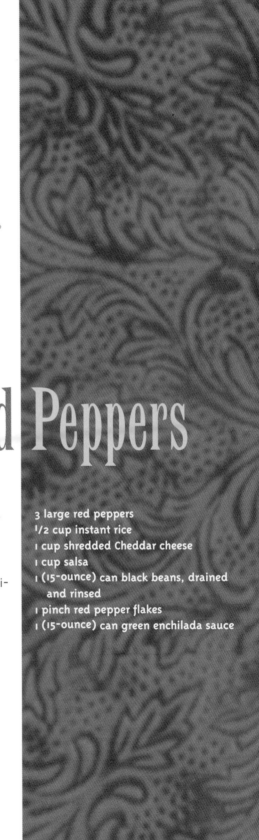

# Vegetarian Stuffed Peppers

Cut the tops off the peppers. Remove the seeds and membranes. In a bowl, stir together the rice, cheese, salsa, beans, and red pepper flakes. Stuff each pepper with the mixture, place in the slow cooker, cover, and cook on low for 3 to 4 hours.

After the rice is tender, cover the peppers with the green enchilada sauce. Turn the slow cooker to high and cook for 20 to 30 minutes or until sauce is warm. • Makes 3 servings

3 large red peppers
1/2 cup instant rice
1 cup shredded Cheddar cheese
1 cup salsa
1 (15-ounce) can black beans, drained and rinsed
1 pinch red pepper flakes
1 (15-ounce) can green enchilada sauce

Coring onions sounds easier than it actually is. The best way to do this is to cut the top off the onion, and then slice, in a circular motion, approximately 1-2 inches deep into the onion, making sure not to cut through the bottom. Next, cut the circle you created into quarters. Carefully pull out any loose pieces of onion. Make another circular cut around the remaining portion of interior onion, and repeat the process above until the entire center has been removed. You will be removing a lot of onion, so reserve it for another recipe.

# Stuffed Onions with Cheese Sauce

4 medium yellow onions, cored
Salt
Cayenne
2 green chiles, chopped
1 (16-ounce) can corn, drained
1 cup water
2 tablespoons butter
3 cloves garlic, finely chopped
2 tablespoons all-purpose flour
1/2 teaspoon black pepper
1 cup non-fat milk
1/4 cup shredded mozzarella cheese
1/4 cup shredded Cheddar cheese

Place each cored onion in the middle of a sheet of aluminum foil. Sprinkle a little salt and cayenne in the center of each onion. In a small bowl, mix the chiles and corn. Using a teaspoon, spoon the chile mixture into the center of each onion. Continue until each onion is stuffed. Wrap each onion securely in its own piece of aluminum foil and stack them in the slow cooker. Add the cup of water, cover, and cook on high for 4 to 5 hours.

About 10 minutes before you are ready to serve the stuffed onions, make the sauce. In a medium pan, melt the butter over medium-high heat. Add the garlic and sauté until soft, about 3 to 4 minutes. Slowly stir in the flour, black pepper, and milk. Cook, stirring constantly, until the mixture is thick and frothy. Add the cheese and stir until it is completely melted. Remove from heat and set aside.

Remove the onions from the foil, place on individual plates, and spoon a few tablespoons of the warm cheese sauce over each stuffed onion. Serve immediately. • Makes 4 Servings

Note: Make sure not to use too much cayenne, as the slow cooker will intensify the peppery aspect of the spice. If you wish to add more heat to the onions, you can mix a seeded and chopped serrano or habanero chile into the corn mixture.

This is a spin on a traditional Spanish dish. The addition of hearty vegetables and a little shredded cheese makes this rice a healthy alternative to your everyday tacos.

# Paella Roja

Place all of the ingredients except for the taco shells and the cheese in the slow cooker. Mix well. Cover and cook on low for 6 to 8 hours or until the rice and zucchini are tender. Spoon 2 to 3 tablespoons of rice mixture into each taco shell, sprinkle with shredded cheese, and microwave for approximately 30 seconds so that the cheese melts and the taco shells are more pliable. Serve immediately with a side of chips and fresh salsa.

• Makes 6-8 Servings

1 medium onion, chopped
4 cloves garlic, chopped
2 habaneros, seeded and diced
1 zucchini, cut in half lengthwise and
    thinly sliced
1 green pepper, seeded and chopped
1 (16-ounce) can green peas, drained
1 (16-ounce) can corn, drained
1 (28-ounce) can peeled
    tomatoes, undrained
1 (8-ounce) can tomato sauce
1 cup water
1 cup converted rice
2 teaspoons cayenne
1 teaspoon salt
2 teaspoons Worcestershire sauce
2 bay leaves
16 hard taco shells
1 cup shredded mozzarella cheese

The first time I had these tasty burritos was on the beach in Mexico. They were hot, smooth, and bursting with flavor. Try them next time you want something other than the typical bean burrito.

# Potato Burritos

5-6 medium red potatoes, quartered
1 package taco seasoning
2 cups water
Shredded lettuce
1/2 medium red onion, chopped
3-4 Roma tomatoes
8 (8-inch) flour tortillas
Salsa
Sour cream

Place the quartered potatoes in the slow cooker. In a separate bowl, mix the water and the package of taco seasoning. Pour over the potatoes. Cover and cook on low for 6 to 8 hours.

Remove the seasoned potatoes and divide into eight equal portions. To make the burritos, take one tortilla, place a portion of the potatoes in the middle, top with tomatoes, onions, and lettuce, and roll. Repeat with remaining ingredients. To serve, place 1 or 2 burritos on each plate, top with a little salsa and a dollop of sour cream, and serve immediately. • Makes 4-6 Servings

We've adapted this recipe from one that the spirited cook, Doña Estela, taught us in Mexico. Don't be afraid to get your hands in there and really mash those potatoes.

# Spinach & Potato Pancakes

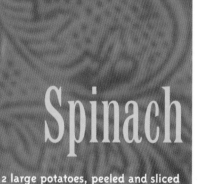

2 large potatoes, peeled and sliced
2 garlic cloves, chopped
2 cups chicken stock
1 cup chopped spinach leaves
1 onion, chopped
1/2 cup crumbled feta cheese
2 eggs
Salt and black pepper
1/2 cup vegetable oil

Place potatoes, garlic, and chicken stock in the slow cooker. Cover and cook on high for 4 to 5 hours. When potatoes are soft, roughly mash and add remaining ingredients, except for the oil.

Mix well with your hands and form mixture into patties about 1/2-inch thick and 3 inches wide. Fry in hot oil until they are golden brown on both sides. Remove from the skillet and drain on a paper towel. Serve with salsa and slices of avocado. • Makes 8 Servings

This twist on a traditional dish can be served for breakfast, lunch, or dinner! It is the ultimate choice when it comes to versatility.

# Chile Relleno Casserole

Spray the inside of your slow cooker with nonstick cooking spray. Cut each poblano into 1/2-inch strips, making sure to remove the seeds and membranes. Set aside.

In a separate bowl, combine the eggs, cream, salt, and flour. Beat until smooth. In the slow cooker, layer the strips of poblano and the cheeses. Repeat until you have approximately three layers. Slowly pour the egg mixture over the chiles and cheese. Cover and cook on low for 4 to 5 hours, or until the egg mixture is cooked through. Carefully turn the crock upside-down to remove the casserole. Cut into individual pieces and serve with salsa and sour cream. • Makes 4 Servings

Nonstick cooking spray
3-4 large poblano chiles
4 eggs
3/4 cup heavy whipping cream
1 teaspoon salt
1/2 cup all-purpose flour
1 cup shredded Monterey Jack cheese
1 cup shredded Cheddar cheese
Salsa
Sour cream

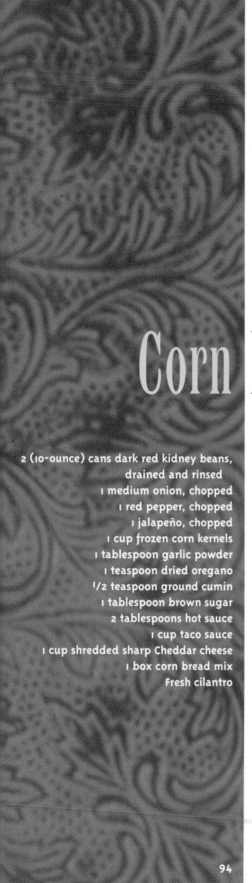

Beans and corn bread are a match made in heaven. This delicious meal will have people coming back for seconds. Buy your favorite corn bread mix. You will probably need an egg and milk to make the batter.

# Corn Bread Casserole

2 (10-ounce) cans dark red kidney beans,
drained and rinsed
1 medium onion, chopped
1 red pepper, chopped
1 jalapeño, chopped
1 cup frozen corn kernels
1 tablespoon garlic powder
1 teaspoon dried oregano
1/2 teaspoon ground cumin
1 tablespoon brown sugar
2 tablespoons hot sauce
1 cup taco sauce
1 cup shredded sharp Cheddar cheese
1 box corn bread mix
Fresh cilantro

Gently mix together all of the ingredients except for the cheese, corn bread mix, and cilantro in your slow cooker. Cover and cook on low for 3 to 4 hours.

Mix together the corn bread batter. While batter is setting, cover the beans with the cheese. When batter is firm, pour over the top of the beans and cheese. Cover and cook on high for 30 minutes, or until the corn bread is cooked through. Top each serving with cilantro. • Makes 4-6 Servings

While cooking in the slow cooker, the edges of this deliciously simple quiche brown and form an almost-crust. This is perfect for breakfast or for lunch.

# Southwest Quiche

Nonstick cooking spray
8 eggs, beaten
1/4 cup all-purpose flour
1/4 cup melted butter or margarine
2 cups shredded Monterey jack cheese
1/2 cup diced roasted green chiles

Generously coat the bottom and sides of the slow cooker with cooking spray. In a separate bowl, thoroughly mix remaining ingredients together and pour into the slow cooker. Cover and cook on low for 3 to 4 hours.

While the quiche is still in the slow cooker, slice into four slices and carefully remove with a spatula. Serve with fresh salsa.

• Makes 4 servings

When was the last time you made home-cooked mashed potatoes or turned a bag of dried beans into a delicious Southwest dish? These recipes under normal circumstances would take hours to make, but the slow cooker changes all of that! Now you can actually cook vegetables the way they were meant to be cooked.

 # Side Dishes

## Acompañamientos

Instead of potato salad, bring these potatoes to your next summer picnic—you'll be the hit of the party!

# Perfect Potatoes

4 to 6 medium red potatoes, quartered
6 slices bacon, cooked and crumbled
1/2 medium-sized red onion, chopped
Salt and freshly ground black pepper
1 tablespoon dried oregano
1 teaspoon cayenne
1 1/2 cups water
1/4 pound butter

Add the potatoes, bacon, onion, salt, pepper, oregano, cayenne, and water to the slow cooker. Slice butter and add to the top of the potatoes. Cover and cook on low for 6 hours, or until the potatoes are tender. • Makes 4-6 Servings

Once again, the slow cooker has come to the rescue! Potatoes take so long to cook that I hardly ever made mashed potatoes. Now, you can let the potatoes cook all day, and then whip up a batch of delicious garlic mashed potatoes in minutes. You can substitute the chicken broth for beef or vegetable broth if you prefer.

# Garlic Mashed Potatoes

Place the potato chunks and the chicken broth in the slow cooker. Cover and cook on low for 6 to 8 hours. When the potatoes are nice and tender, remove from the slow cooker and discard the liquid. In a large bowl, lightly mash the potatoes with a potato masher. Add the green chiles, garlic powder, black pepper, and butter. Mix well, and mash to desired consistency. Serve immediately.
● Makes 6-8 Servings

3 large Russet potatoes, peeled and cut into chunks
6 cups chicken broth
2 green chiles
1/2 tablespoon garlic powder
1/2 teaspoon black pepper
4 tablespoons butter

This recipe is creamy and delicious. The secret is to not overcook it. You don't want the cheese and milk to separate.

# Creamed Corn with Chiles

In your slow cooker, whisk together all of the ingredients except for the corn and green chiles. When thoroughly mixed, stir in the corn and chiles. Cover and cook on low for 3 to 4 hours. Stir occasionally. ● Makes 4-6 Servings

1 tablespoon butter
1/2 cup shredded Monterey jack cheese
1 cup milk
2 teaspoons salt
1 teaspoon sugar
1 teaspoon cayenne
2 tablespoons all-purpose flour
1 (16-ounce) bag frozen corn kernels
2 green chiles, roasted, seeded, and chopped

Every time I eat carrots I think about how good they are for you. I can practically feel my eyesight getting better. It's a great feeling, so I eat them whenever I can. This is an excellent side dish with pork or chicken. Toasting the cumin seeds brings out a their rich flavor.

# Carrots with Toasted Cumin

7 large carrots, peeled and sliced diagonally
3 cloves garlic, crushed
2 teaspoons cumin seeds, toasted
1 tablespoon honey
1 tablespoon olive oil
Salt
Cayenne
1/4 cup chicken stock
Lime juice

Combine all ingredients in the slow cooker. Cover and cook on low for 4 to 6 hours. Fifteen minutes before serving, remove lid and turn heat to high so that remaining liquid evaporates. Immediately before serving, sprinkle with lime juice. • Makes 4-6 Servings

Everyone has a glazed carrot recipe, but this one takes it to the next level! Add as much cayenne as you like, as the spiciness will be mellowed out by the sweet flavors.

# Classic Carrots with a Kick

Freshly squeezed juice from 2 oranges, approximately 1/2 cup
1/2 cup packed brown sugar
1/2 teaspoon ground cinnamon
1/4 teaspoon nutmeg
1/2 teaspoon cayenne
1 cup dry white wine
3 tablespoons butter, melted
1 yellow onion, chopped
Freshly ground black pepper
1 (32-ounce) package peeled baby carrots

Mix all ingredients except the carrots in the slow cooker and stir until well blended. Add the carrots and stir until all carrots are lightly coated. Cover and cook on high for 5 to 6 hours, or until the carrots are tender. This dish is especially good when served with grilled fish or chicken. • Makes 4-6 Servings

This tasty dish is best served during the fall months when squash is fresh. Serve it as a side to baked chicken or fish, or serve it as a vegetarian main course option with rice.

# Sweet Squash

In a medium bowl, mix together the chopped apples, brown sugar, a sprinkle of cinnamon, and a dash of lemon juice. Divide the mixture evenly and stuff each squash half. Place 1/2 tablespoon of butter on top of each filled squash half. Wrap each half in foil, layer in the slow cooker, and add the water to the bottom of the slow cooker. Cook on low for 5 to 6 hours, or until squash is cooked through. Unwrap each squash half and serve warm.

● Makes 2–4 Servings

2 Granny Smith apples, peeled and chopped
1/2 cup packed brown sugar
Cinnamon
Lemon juice
2 acorn squash, cut in half lengthwise
    and seeded
2 tablespoons butter
1/2 cup water

These yams are brilliantly orange, sweet, and spicy. They'll liven up any meal.

# Honey Smashed Yams

2 large yams, peeled and cut into
1/2-inch thick rounds
1 cup chicken stock
1 tablespoon butter or margarine
1/2 teaspoon ground cumin
1/4 teaspoon cayenne
Juice of one lime
3 tablespoons honey
1/2 teaspoon salt

Place sliced yams, stock, and butter in slow cooker. Cover and cook on low for 6 to 7 hours. When yams are tender, smash with a potato masher. Add the remaining ingredients, stir, and serve. Top with sour cream if desired. • Makes 4-5 Servings

Yeehaw! For an authentic cowboy experience, plug your slow cooker in outside and eat these beans under a starry sky. If you're not up for it, your warm toasty kitchen will do.

# Cowboy Beans

1 pound dried pinto beans, rinsed
1 small onion, chopped
1 tablespoon garlic powder
4 bacon slices, cooked and cut
into 1-inch pieces
4 cups water
1 cup barbecue sauce

Cover the beans with water and soak overnight. In the morning, drain and rinse the beans.

Combine the beans with the onion, garlic powder, bacon, and water in the slow cooker. Stir thoroughly. Cover and cook on high for 7 to 8 hours. Stir in the barbecue sauce. Cover and cook on low for 1 to 2 more hours, or until the beans are tender.
• Makes 4-6 Servings

Originally from Bean Town, my family and I ate baked beans and brats on Saturdays. This recipe shakes up the original recipe a bit. These beans have zing and pizzazz but are still as comforting as the baked beans we grew up eating. ✹

# Southwest Baked Beans

Cover beans with water and the vinegar and soak overnight. In the morning, drain and rinse the beans.

Combine all ingredients together in the slow cooker and stir thoroughly. Cover and cook on high for 4 hours. Stir and continue cooking on low for 3 to 4 more hours, or until the beans are tender.

● Makes 4-6 Servings

1 pound small white beans, rinsed
1 tablespoon white vinegar
4 slices bacon, cooked and cut into
   1-inch pieces
3 chipotle chiles in adobo sauce, seeded
   and chopped
2 tablespoons adobo sauce (from
   canned chipotles)
1 large onion, chopped
3 cloves garlic, crushed
1/2 cup ketchup
1 (12-ounce) can beer
1/4 cup packed brown sugar
1 tablespoon mustard
1 teaspoon ground cumin
2 1/2 cups water

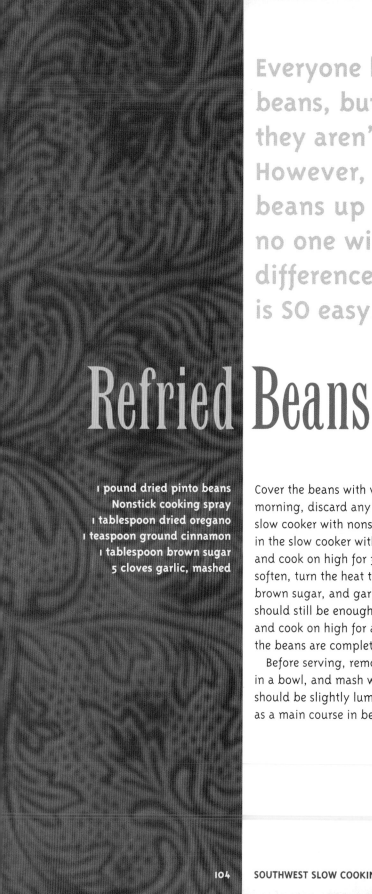

Everyone has had refried beans, but in the slow cooker, they aren't actually "refried." However, if you put these beans up to the real thing, no one will be able to tell the difference, and this method is SO easy!

# Refried Beans

1 pound dried pinto beans
Nonstick cooking spray
1 tablespoon dried oregano
1 teaspoon ground cinnamon
1 tablespoon brown sugar
5 cloves garlic, mashed

Cover the beans with water and soak them overnight. In the morning, discard any floaters and rinse. Spray the inside of the slow cooker with nonstick cooking spray. Place the rinsed beans in the slow cooker with enough water to cover by 1 inch. Cover and cook on high for 3 to 4 hours. After the beans have started to soften, turn the heat to low and add the oregano, cinnamon, brown sugar, and garlic. Add more water if necessary (there should still be enough to barely cover the beans). Mix well. Cover and cook on high for approximately 4 to 5 hours more, or until the beans are completely soft.

Before serving, remove the beans from the slow cooker, place in a bowl, and mash with a potato masher. The consistency should be slightly lumpy but well mixed. Serve as a side dish or as a main course in bean burritos. • Makes 6-8 Servings

From breads to crisps to cakes, this chapter contains all you'll need to finish off a good meal. Indulge yourself!

 # Breads & Desserts Pan y Postres

This bread can be served for breakfast or dessert and is excellent when served with sliced strawberries and whipped cream.

# Banana Bread

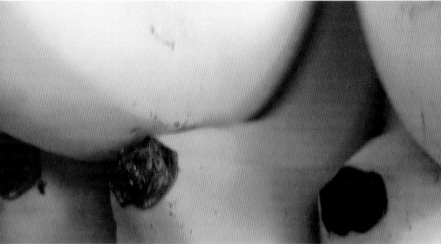

Nonstick cooking spray
3/4 cup sugar
2 tablespoons butter or margarine, softened
1 egg
3/4 cup milk
3 cups all-purpose flour
3 1/2 teaspoons baking powder
1 teaspoon salt
1 cup mashed bananas
3/4 cup chopped nuts

Thoroughly coat a 2 1/2-pound coffee can with nonstick cooking spray. Mix sugar, butter, and egg thoroughly. Slowly stir in milk. Add flour, baking powder, salt, and bananas, and combine until all ingredients are well blended. Stir in nuts. Pour into greased can. Cover can with foil and place in the slow cooker. Cover and cook on high for 2 to 4 hours. Let cool for 10 minutes before removing from can. ● Makes 6-8 Servings

This bread makes the perfect accompaniment to any Southwest meal. The green chiles offer an unexpected flavor. And your guests won't believe that it came out of a slow cooker!

# Green Chile Corn Bread

Coat the inside bottom and sides of the slow cooker with cooking spray. In a large bowl, mix the cornmeal, all-purpose flour, whole wheat flour, baking powder, baking soda, and salt. Stir until well blended. In a medium-sized bowl, beat the eggs, buttermilk, molasses, and margarine. Slowly add to the dry mixture, and stir until well blended. Add the chiles, green onions, and the cheese. Mix well. Slowly pour the mixture into the greased slow cooker.

Cover and cook on high for 2 hours, or until the bread is cooked through. Allow bread to cool for 10 minutes, and then turn the slow cooker upside-down to remove the bread. Allow to cool for 5 more minutes before cutting. Serve warm with your favorite Southwest soup or stew. • Makes 6-8 Servings

Note: To check for doneness, insert a toothpick in the center of the bread. When the toothpick comes out clean, the bread is done.

Nonstick cooking spray
1 cup yellow cornmeal
3/4 cup all-purpose flour
1/2 cup whole wheat flour
1 1/2 teaspoons baking powder
1/2 teaspoon baking soda
1/4 teaspoon salt
2 eggs
1 1/4 cups buttermilk
2 tablespoons molasses
1/4 cup butter or margarine, melted
2 green chiles, roasted and chopped
3 green onions, chopped
2 cups shredded sharp Cheddar cheese

Pine nuts and pumpkins are plentiful in the Southwest during the fall months. This bread is a delicious way to pay homage to these wonderful Native American staples.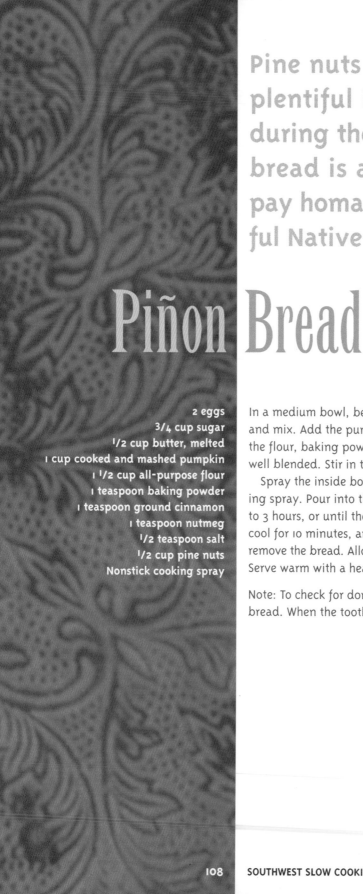

# Piñon Bread

2 eggs
3/4 cup sugar
1/2 cup butter, melted
1 cup cooked and mashed pumpkin
1 1/2 cup all-purpose flour
1 teaspoon baking powder
1 teaspoon ground cinnamon
1 teaspoon nutmeg
1/2 teaspoon salt
1/2 cup pine nuts
Nonstick cooking spray

In a medium bowl, beat the eggs. Add the sugar and the butter and mix. Add the pumpkin and mix again until well blended. Add the flour, baking powder, cinnamon, nutmeg, and salt. Mix until well blended. Stir in the pine nuts.

Spray the inside bottom and sides of the slow cooker with cooking spray. Pour into the slow cooker, cover, and cook on high for 2 to 3 hours, or until the bread is cooked through. Allow bread to cool for 10 minutes, and then turn the slow cooker upside-down to remove the bread. Allow to cool for 5 more minutes before cutting. Serve warm with a hearty fall entrée. • Makes 6-8 Servings

Note: To check for doneness, insert a toothpick in the center of the bread. When the toothpick comes out clean, the bread is done.

This is an extremely versatile dessert. You can serve it alone, on top of vanilla ice cream, or even inside your next homemade pie. But be assured that no matter how you serve it, your guests will be amazed this dish came from a slow cooker.

# Apples Delight

Place the apple slices in the slow cooker. Top with the lemon slices. In a medium-sized mixing bowl, mix the wine, cinnamon, nutmeg, sugar, and brown sugar until well blended. Slowly pour the mixture over the apple and lemon slices, making sure that the apples are well coated. Cover and cook on high for 2 to 3 hours. Remove from slow cooker and allow to cool slightly. Spoon the apples into individual serving bowls and top with vanilla ice cream. • Makes 8-12 Servings

6 Granny Smith apples, peeled, cored, and each cut into 8 slices
1 lemon, cut into thin slices
2 cups red wine
1 tablespoon ground cinnamon
1 teaspoon nutmeg
1/4 cup sugar
1/2 cup light brown sugar
Vanilla ice cream

This has always been a staple dessert in our home every peach season. It's so simple, yet irresistible. People will try to guess what that secret ingredient is—don't tell them.

# Peach Cobbler

Nonstick cooking spray
6 large peaches, peeled and cut into pieces
1 tablespoon sugar
1 1/2 cups yellow cake mix
1/3 cup butter, melted

Coat the bottom and sides of your slow cooker with cooking spray. Spread the peaches evenly in the slow cooker and sprinkle with sugar. Sprinkle the cake mix over the peaches. Drizzle the butter evenly over the cake mix. Cover and cook on high for 2 hours. Serve hot. • Makes 6–8 Servings

These spiced peaches are an after-dinner treat in the Southwest. In the early fall, the peaches are perfectly ripe and juicy, and the spiciness reminds you of a crisp, autumn day.

# Spiced Peaches

3 peaches, peeled, pitted, and each cut into approximately 8 slices
2 tablespoons packed brown sugar
1/2 cinnamon stick
Pinch of nutmeg
2 whole cloves
1/3 cup brandy

Combine the peaches, sugar, cinnamon, nutmeg, cloves, and brandy in the slow cooker. Stir until well blended and the peaches are coated. Cover and cook on low for 4 to 5 hours. When peaches are tender, remove the cloves and cinnamon stick. Chill the peaches and sauce for at least 1 hour before serving. The sauce will thicken as the peaches cool. Serve in individual stemmed glasses or over vanilla ice cream. • Makes 4-6 Servings

Arroz con leche is a classic dessert served in many Latin American countries. Popular with both children and parents, it is sweet, soothing, and smooth—a delicate blend of spice and cream. Arroz con leche can be served warm or cold, depending on your personal preference.

# Arroz con Leche

Combine 4 1/2 cups of the milk, rice, sugar, raisins, butter, salt, cinnamon stick, and vanilla in the slow cooker. Stir well. Cover and cook on low for 2 1/2 hours, stirring every 30 minutes.

In a separate bowl, stir together the remaining 1/2 cup of milk with the egg substitute. Thoroughly stir together with the hot rice in the slow cooker. Add sour cream and lime zest.

Turn off the slow cooker and let the rice pudding cool for about 20 minutes. Remove and discard the cinnamon stick. Separate the rice pudding into separate serving bowls and chill in the refrigerator for 2 or more hours. Serve cold with ground cinnamon sprinkled over the top. • Makes 6-8 Servings

4 1/2 cups plus 1/2 cup milk
1 cup uncooked converted rice
1 cup sugar
1 cup raisins
2 tablespoons butter, melted
1/2 teaspoon salt
1 stick cinnamon
1 tablespoon vanilla extract
1/4 cup liquid egg substitute
1/2 cup sour cream
1/2 teaspoon lime zest
Ground cinnamon

Everyone loves chocolate, so this fondue is the perfect way to top off an evening with friends and family. It is so easy to prepare, and the cinnamon gives the dip a little hint of South-of-the-border mystique. This fondue is especially good when served with fresh strawberries, bananas, and pound cake.

# Mexican Chocolate Fondue

1/2 cup heavy whipping cream
1 (12-ounce) package semisweet chocolate chips
2 tablespoons cinnamon schnapps

Mix all ingredients in the slow cooker until well blended. Cover and cook on low for 1 to 2 hours, or until the chocolate is fully melted. Stir often. • Makes 4-6 Servings

When fall rolls in and apples are in season, serve this gooey and delicious dip with your favorite apple variety. The Kahlua adds a roasted coffee flavor and the caramel makes this dip deliriously sweet. It will go fast, but it's impossible not to smile between bites.

# Caramel Kahlua Fondue

Cook caramels and cream on low for 2 hours. Stir in marshmallows and Kahlua and continue to cook for 30 minutes, or until dipping sauce is completely melted. Stir and serve with sliced apples.
• Makes 4-6 Servings

2 cups unwrapped chewy caramel candies
1/2 cup cream
1/2 cup miniature marshmallows
1 tablespoon Kahlua
5 apples, sliced

Growing up, this was my favorite dessert. It is by far the best chocolate cake I have ever tasted. You can use store-bought cream cheese frosting to shorten the process, but making your own is so rewarding...and it just tastes better! Thanks, Mom, for this timeless recipe.

# Chocolate Cake with Cream Cheese Frosting

**Cake:**
2 cups all-purpose flour
1 teaspoon baking soda
1 1/2 cups sugar
1/4 teaspoon salt
6 tablespoons cocoa powder
1 egg or 1/4 cup Egg Beaters®
1 cup "real" mayonnaise
1 cup hot water
1 teaspoon vanilla
Nonstick cooking spray

**Frosting:**
2 1/2 cups powdered sugar
4 ounces cream cheese, softened
1/2 teaspoon vanilla
Approximately 1/2 cup milk

In a large mixing bowl, stir together the dry cake ingredients. Add the remaining cake ingredients and beat for 2 minutes with an electric mixer. Coat a 2 1/2-pound coffee can with cooking spray and then lightly flour it. Pour the cake mix into the can and cover with foil. Place in the slow cooker, cover, and bake on high for 2 to 3 hours, or until done. Let cool for 10 minutes, and then remove from the can.

To make the frosting, mix the sugar, cream cheese, and vanilla with an electric mixer until smooth. Add the milk slowly until the frosting is a good spreading consistency. Beat until very smooth. Spread the frosting generously on the cooled cake and serve for any occasion! • Makes 8-10 Servings

Apples are grown all over the Southwest, so add a pinch of cinnamon, a few spicy cloves, and experience a true taste of fall with this fresh applesauce cake.

# Applesauce Cake

1 1/2 cups sugar
1/2 cup margarine
2 eggs or 1/2 cup Egg Beaters®
2 cups sweetened applesauce
3 cups all-purpose flour
1/2 teaspoon salt
2 teaspoons ground cinnamon
1 teaspoon ground cloves
1/2 teaspoon allspice
1 3/4 teaspoons baking soda
1 cup finely chopped walnuts
Nonstick cooking spray

In a medium bowl, mix the sugar and margarine. Add the eggs and beat well. In a separate bowl, sift the dry ingredients together, and then add alternately with the applesauce to the egg mixture. Mix well. Stir in the nuts. Coat a 2 1/2-pound coffee can with cooking spray and pour the cake batter into the can. Bake in a covered slow cooker on high for approximately 3 1/2 hours, or until done. • Makes 6-8 Servings

The green chiles in this recipe give this apple crisp an authentic Southwest flair—it is amazing how well the flavors complement each other.

# Chile Apple Crisp

Filling:
3 Granny Smith apples, peeled, cored, and thinly sliced
3 Gala apples, peeled, cored, and thinly sliced
1 tablespoon lemon juice
1/2 cup raw sugar
3 tablespoons all-purpose flour
2 tablespoons cinnamon
1/2 teaspoon nutmeg
2 green chiles, roasted, peeled, seeded, and chopped
1/2 cup water

Topping:
2 tablespoons plus 1 tablespoon butter
2 cups granola
1/4 cup brown sugar

In your slow cooker, toss together all of the filling ingredients except for the water. When apples are coated, add water and stir. Cover and cook on high for 2 hours.

In the meantime, melt 2 tablespoons of the butter in a skillet. Lightly brown the granola in the butter, stirring frequently, about 10 minutes. Set aside. After two hours, stir the apples and cover with the granola. Dot the remaining butter on top of the granola and sprinkle with brown sugar. Cover and continue cooking on high for 15 minutes. Serve warm with vanilla ice cream. • Makes 6-8 Servings

# Acknowledgements

This project would not have been successful without the help of some very important people. We would first like to thank our wonderful husbands, Brian and Dave, for their unending patience and support. We couldn't have made it through this process without your consistent encouragement and honest input.

Also, to our loving families, Susan, Carl, and Emily Schnapp, Tim D. and Tim M. Gales, and Katie and Jake Wadsley, we thank you for standing behind us on this venture and for teaching us the importance of a home-cooked meal. You gave us the strength and dedication to see this project through to completion. And to Mary Gales, we thank you for your invaluable help. Without all your advice and innovative ideas along the way, this book would not be complete.

We would like to thank our darling pets, Suyani, Chuska, Zoey, and Samson, who love us no matter what.

Many thanks also go to all of the amazing people who volunteered to recreate our recipes in their own homes. To Diane Cavis, Debby VanStratten, Rose Spindler, and Sandy Burkhardt, we greatly appreciate the time and effort you put into testing our recipes, as well as your valuable comments and feedback.

To Doña Estela and Señor John at Mexican Home Cooking in Tlaxcala, we offer you a big muchas gracias! You taught us that there is so much more to cooking than the ingredients. Thank you for sharing your home and your cooking philosophies. We are grateful.

Finally, we would like to thank our fellow Northland Publishing team for giving us the opportunity to publish this book. To Kathleen Bryant, we thank you for the meticulous editing job. To Dave Jenney, Katie Jennings, and Donna Boyd, we thank you for all of your creativity along the way. This has been a great project, and we sincerely had fun sharing it with all of you.

# Index

*Note: Italicized numbers indicate photographs*

# Index

# Index